Tintern Abbey, Monmouthshire

A

Walk though Wales,

IN AUGUST 1797,

BY THE

Rev^d. Richard Warner,

OF BATH.

Σα γαρ εϛι κεινα παντα.

"Creation's tenant! all the world is thine."

London
Hounskull Publishing
2024

HOUNSKULL PUBLISHING
BM Box Hounskull
London WC1N 3XX

A Walk through Wales, in August 1797
Originally published in 1798

First Hounskull edition published 2024
© Hounskull Publishing 2024

ISBN 978-1-910893-29-6

Table of Contents

Note on This Edition
ix

Advertisement
xi

Itinerary
xiii

Letter I
1

Letter II
21

Letter III
37

Letter IV
51

Letter V
65

Letter VI
75

Letter VII
87

Letter VIII
105

Letter IX
117

Letter X
131

Letter XI
139

Letter XII
153

TABLE OF CONTENTS

Letter XIII
167

Letter XIV
175

Letter XV
183

Letter XVI
189

Letter XVII
197

Letter XVIII
203

Index
211

Note on This Edition

The present volume is based on the 1798 edition published in London by C. Dilly. The text has been reproduced in its entirety.

The spelling, punctuation and and capitalisation have been left as in the original. The titles of works mentioned have been taken out of quotation marks and put in italics. Also put in italics have been passages in Latin where they appeared in Roman in the text. Geographical names that appeared in the original with alternative spellings have been indexed with the accepted modern spelling, except when the latter has not been found.

A number of editorial footnotes have been added and identified as such. A full index has been generated.

Advertisement

he following letters were written to a friend during a Walk through Wales in August last. Since that time, they have been added to and corrected; and are now presented to the public, under the impression, that they may be found to afford some few hints and observations not altogether useless to those whose curiosity shall lead them to visit the very striking scenery of North-Wales. The route of each day is engraven, and prefixed to the letter that contains a detail of its events; in which little sketches the more considerable deviations from the public road, made in order to visit particular objects, are marked with dotted lines. These are intended for the direction of the Pedestrian, whose independent mode of travelling enables him to catch beauties in his walk through an Alpine country, which the incumbrance of a carriage, and even the indulgence of a horse, prevents another traveller from enjoying.

BATH, JANUARY 1798

Itinerary

		Miles	
		Miles	
Monday, Aug. 14th, 1797	From Bath to the New-Passage	24	
	Across the Severn	3	
	Caerwent	3	
	Usk	9	− 39
Tuesday, 15th	Abergavenny	11	
	Crickhowel	6	
	Brecon	13	− 30
Wednesday, 16th	Bualt	15	
	Rhaiddar	17	− 32
Thursday, 17th	Pentre	15	
	Havod	2	

	Devil's Bridge including Havod grounds	6	— 23
Friday, 18th	Machynyllyth over the mountains	25	— 25
Saturday, 19th	Talyllyn	8	
	Dolgelly over Cader-Idris	16	— 24
Sunday, 20th	Dol-y-Myllyn fall	6	
	Cayne and Mouddach fall	4	
	Tan-y-Bwlch	10	
	Bethgelert	8	— 28
Monday, 21st	Round and over Snowdon to Dolbadern Castle	17	
	Caernarvon	8	— 25
Tuesday, 22d	Bangor	9	
	Conway	15	
	Round Caernarvon	1½	—25½
Wednesday, 23d	Llawnrwst	12	
	Capel Voelas	10	
	Cernioge	2	
	Round Conway	1½	—25½
Thursday, 24th	Corwen	13	
	Llangollen	10	— 23
Friday, 25th	Valle-Crucis, Dinas-Bran, and back	6	
	Oswestry	12	
	Llanymynach	6	— 24
Saturday, 26th	Welsh-Pool by Canal	12	
	Montgomery by Powis Castle	8	— 20
Sunday, 27th	Clun	12	
	Pentre-Audrey	4	
	Bucknell	2	
	Brampton-Brian	2	

LETTER I

	Wigmore	4	— 24
Monday, 28th	Round Wigmore, Castle, &c.	1	
	Mortimer's Cross	3	
	Hereford	19	— 23
Tuesday, 29th	Wilton by the banks of the Wye	20	— 20
Wednesday, 30th	Goodrich Castle	3	
	New Weir	2	
	Doward	2	
	Monmouth	3	
	Redbrook	2	
	Llandogo	4	
	Tintern ferry	4	— 20
Thursday, 31st	Chepstow by the Wine Cliff	6	
	New Passage	5	
	Across the Severn	3	
	Bath	24	— 38
			469

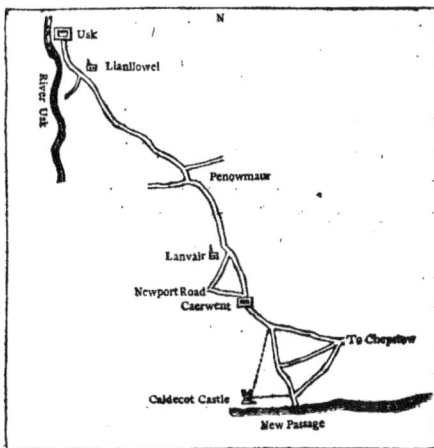

N

Usk

Llanllowel

River Usk

Penowmaur

Lanvair

Newport Road

Caerwent

To Chepstow

Caldecot Castle

New Passage

Letter I

DEAR SIR   Usk, Aug. 14th, 1797

You will not be astonished at receiving a letter from the northern side of the Severn, apprised as you were of my intention to perambulate Wales in the course of this month.

An expedition of this nature, you know, has often been the subject of our conversation, long before I became an inhabitant of a place so immediately in the neighbourhood of the Principality; and, even when strolling through the glades of New Forest, we have more than once amused ourselves with anticipating the pleasure we should receive, when leisure and opportunity would allow us to visit the country of the ancient Britons; to wander along the sweet banks of the Dovy; to climb the steeps of Snowdon and Cader Idris; to listen to the thundering cataracts of Mouddach and Dol-y-Myllyn; to admire the variegated landscapes of Festiniogg, Clwyd, and Langollen; and to breathe the inspiring air where liberty made her last stand in these kingdoms, against the strides of Roman power, under the gallant Silurian and Ordovician chieftains.

The particular circumstances which prevented you from being my companion, induced me to drop the idea of this pilgrimage last year; and as they still continued to operate, I should probably have suffered this autumn also to elapse without performing it, had not C——— expressed a wish to accompany me. I before mentioned to you his offer, and the readiness with which I accepted such an agreeable associate. Solitary pleasures are, at the best, but imperfect; and with respect to travelling in particular, the gratification arising from it depends so much upon having a companion, with whom one can interchange sentiment, and communicate observation, as leads me entirely to coincide with Cicero in thinking, that even a journey to the stars without society would be but a dull kind of expedition.[1]

---

1   *Verumergo id est; si quis in cœlum ascendisset, naturam-que mundi, et pulchritudinem siderûm perspexisset, insu-*

In preparing for a pedestrian tour, few arrangements are requisite: a single change of raiment, and some other little articles for the comfort of the person, form all the necessary baggage of a foot-traveller. To convey these, however, light as they may be, in the most easy and convenient manner, is an object of importance, and requires some previous thought and consideration. C——, conceiving it might be best effected by the assistance of side-pockets, has had two receptacles of this kind, of considerable dimensions, added to his coat. My plan is a different one: a neglected Spencer, which, though somewhat threadbare and rusty, may still make a respectable figure in North Wales, has, by the taylor's skill, been fitted up with a sportsman's pocket, that sweeps from one side to the other, and allows room sufficient for all the articles necessary to be carried.[2]

---

avem illam admirationem ei fore, quæ jucundissima fuisset, sialiquemcui narraret habuisset. DE AMIC.

2 Experience has since convinced us, that both these modes of carrying necessaries are exceptionable, and by no means so commodious as a method we observed to have been adopted by a pedestrian party, which we encountered in Cardiganshire. Each of the gentlemen (for there were three of them) carried a handsome leathern bag, covered with neat network, which, being suspended from the right shoulder by a strap, hung under the left arm, in the manner of a shooting-bag. This was occasionally shifted from one shoulder to the other, and at the same time that it proved a most convenient conveyance for linen, &c. was no inelegant addition to the person; at least, it gave the wearer much less the appearance of a pedlar than attached to us, from the enormous side pockets of my companion, and my own swoln Spencer.

Accoutred in this manner, and provided with maps and a compass, which we understand are indispensably requisite amongst the mountains of Merioneth and Caernarvonshire, we left Bath this morning as the clock was striking five. There is something wonderfully inspiriting in the commencement of a journey to a place which we have never before visited. The mind, delighting in novelty, eagerly anticipates the gratification, which scenes that are new to it are found to afford; and the imagination, always alive and active, when its creative powers are not restrained by previous knowledge, is busied in painting fancied beauties, and forming ideal pleasures, which are never discovered in the real picture, nor experienced in actual enjoyment.

We were in high spirits; and the beauty of the opening day added to our hilarity. Every circumstance that could cheer or enliven, was present to us:

> The attemper'd sun arose
> Sweet-beam'd, and shedding oft through lucid clouds
> A pleasing calm—

A gentle western breeze, that seemed to bring

It is proper to note also, that, in addition to our stock of necessaries, we each found it convenient to provide ourselves with a small drinking-horn; for although we had no difficulty in procuring milk, and other sorts of beverage, yet the vessels from which we quaffed these potations were not always so clean as those we had been accustomed to use.

health and pleasure on its wings, played around us; the hills echoed the thousand "melodies of-morn;" the woods rang with harmony; and we confessed that the animated description of the poet was not the language of fiction:

But who the melodies of morn can tell?
The wild brook babbling down the mountain side;
The lowing herd; the sheepfold's simple bell;
The pipe of early shepherd dim descried
In the lone valley; echoing far and wide
The clamorous horn along the cliffs above;
The hollow murmur of the ocean-tide;
The hum of bees, and linnets' lay of love,
And the full choir that wakes the universal grove.

The cottage-curs at early pilgrim bark;
Crown'd with her pail the tripping milk-maid sings;
The whistling plowman stalks afield; and hark!
Down the rough slope the ponderous waggon rings;
Through rustling corn the hare astonish'd springs;
Slow tolls the village clock the drowsy hour;
The partridge bursts away on whirring wings;
Deep mourns the turtle in sequester'd bower,
And shrill lark carols clear from her aërial tour.
BEATTIE'S MINSTREL.

As we were desirous to avoid Bristol, for our object is neither "tower'd cities," nor "the busy hum of men," we passed it on the left, and continued our walk to Westbury, a village about fifteen miles from Bath. Here the sign of the Goat caught our attention, and considering it as a propitious omen, and emblematic of the expedition in which we are engaged, we determined to breakfast under its venerable figure; though the house, from which it hung as a signal of invitation to the passing traveller, did not appear to be such as would afford us very sumptuous fare. Nor, indeed, did its externals deceive us; the milk was thin, the bread stale, and the water half cold; but such is the magical operation of kind attention and a willingness to oblige, that notwithstanding these little defects in our entertainment, we left the Goat in as perfect harmony of temper with its civil mistress and her attentive handmaid, as if they had spread before us the substantial cream and relishing *sally-luns* of Sydney-Gardens.

No circumstance worth observation occurred till we were within a mile of the New Passage, when, hearing the rattling of a carriage, we turned round, and perceived we should soon be overtaken by a cart which contained two fashionable young females. I am sorry to confess, my friend, that philosophers as we are, we felt confounded at the idea of being discovered by so smart a party, on foot, in the turnpike-road, and equipped as I have described ourselves to be; nor was our confusion lessened, when we perceived that one of the ladies was a distant acquaintance of each of us. I must also acknowledge, that this emotion of false shame and I had was the more unpardonable, as C—— and I had before worked ourselves, by divers arguments and much reasoning, into a fancied heroism in this respect; having

6

been aware that such trials of vanity might befal us, and having coolly discussed the absurdity of allowing them to gall our feelings, or wound our pride. The moment, however, that the enquiring eye of Miss —— surveyed us,—*ibi omnis effusus labor*—our philosophy vanished into air; our laboured reasonings fell to the ground; our fancied heroism flew off in a tangent, and we found that speculation and practice were not quite so necessarily connected together as cause and effect.

Before we reached the Passage, however, we had again recovered our senses, and acquired a sufficient degree of confidence to accost the ladies, whom we saw on the beach. It now appeared, (and we were not a little amused at the discovery) that *they* had been as much distressed at being seen riding in a cart, as we were, walking in the public road, with our wallets at our backs. Mutual explanations took place. They assured us, they had *ventured* to *ascend* the ignoble machine, because it was the *only vehicle* which could be procured in the village where they lodged; and we declared we had chosen to walk through Wales, because we were *passionately fond* of the exercise, and avoided, by adopting that plan, the care, trouble, and inconvenience of *horses* and *carriages*.

We now took leave of the ladies, and proceeded to the packet, into which we did not get admission without considerable difficulty, the boatmen having taken advantage of our being engaged in conversation, and actually put off from the shore without us, although we had previously spoken for a passage. This is a common manœuvre with the very barbarous description of beings who ply the vessels engaged in crossing the Severn; a trick that obliges the disappointed traveller to engage a boat for himself, at the expence of six shillings, instead of nine-pence. The boats being all one joint concern, the oftener this can be effected the more the interest of the proprietors is served, and, doubtless, the more advantageous it is to the men. Indeed, long as I have lived near maritime towns, and much as I have seen of the nautical character, I never witnessed half the barbarism that shocks one at this place. The sailor, though always a rough and unpolished, is seldom a savage or brutal character; at the New Passage, however, a different species appears, and were we to judge of the *genus* from this particular *class*, the tar would sink much in our estimation. The cause of this exception to a general rule, appears to arise from the circumstance of the Passage being in the hands of a partnership. This being the case, there are, of course, no separate interests; no competitions; no struggle to deserve preference by particular attention, or superior courtesy; no endeavour to engage the future custom of the passenger by consulting his present ease, convenience, or pleasure; no stimulus to ensure civility; no check to prevent insolence; and the consequence is what we may naturally expect it to be, the mariners engaged in the business are as rude, turbulent, and violent, as the æstuary they navigate; each individual resembling the Stygian ferryman, described by Virgil:—

> *Portitor has horrendus aquas et flumina servat*
> *Terribili squalore Charon; cui plurima mento*
> *Canities inculta jacet; stant lumina flamma.*
> VIRG. VI. 298.

Whilst crossing the Severn we could not but recollect that we were floating on a river of no ignoble name; a stream famed in British story, and not unnoticed by the classic historians. Tacitus,[3] you know, speaks of the *Sabrina*, and observes, that the proprætor P. Ostorius fortified it with a chain of forts, in order to awe the surrounding parts. In the early writers of our own country this stream makes a conspicuous figure; and the fanciful fable of the origin of its name, which these romancers handed down to posterity, has afforded a subject to our great poet, for some fine lines in his delicious *Comus*:—

> There is a gentle Nymph not far from hence,
> That with moist curb sways the smooth Severn stream,
> Sabrina is her name, a virgin pure;
> Whilome she was the daughter of Locrine,
> That had his sceptre from his father Brute.
> She, guiltless damsel, flying the mad pursuit
> Of her enraged step-dame Guendolen,
> Commended her fair innocence to the flood,

---

3   *Ann.* xii. 31.

That stay'd her flight with his cross-flowing course.
The water-nymphs, that in the bottom play'd,
Held up their pearled wrists, and took her in,
Bearing her strait to aged Nereus' hall,
Who, piteous of her woes, rear'd her lank head,
And gave her to his daughters to imbathe
In nectar'd lavers strew'd with asphodil,
And through the porch and inlet of each sense
Dropt in ambrosial oils, till she reviv'd,
And underwent a quick immortal change,
Made goddess of the river: still she retains
Her maiden gentleness, and oft at eve
Visits the herds along the twilight meads,
Helping all urchin blasts, and ill-luck signs
That the shrewd medling else delights to make,
Which she with precious vial'd liquor heals.

Having crossed the Severn, we now felt ourselves fairly entered upon our expedition. We had passed the great boundary that divides Wales from England, and trod on land, which till lately, made part of the Principality. Quitting the road to Caerwent, we turned to the left, in order to visit the ruins of Caldecot castle, which lay at the distance of a mile in that direction. On our walk thither we could not but remark a profusion of the *absinthium vulgare*, or common wormwood, which flourishes here in great perfection. The uses to which this plant is applied, and the medicinal preparations drawn from it, its conserve, extract, salt, and essential oil, are well known; we were therefore much surprised to understand, on enquiry, that although such quantities are spontaneously produced in the neighbourhood, its virtues were not understood here, and that the plant was suffered to flourish and decay, without regard or attention; a negligence which reminded us of the poet's observation:

> And yet the wholesome herb neglected dies.
> Though with the pure exhilarating soul
> Of nutriment and health, and vital powers,
> Beyond the reach of art, 'tis copious bless'd.
> THOMSON'S *SPRING*.

The ruin of Caldecot castle disappointed us. In its appearance there is nothing striking or picturesque; nor does its situation convey the idea of strength or importance. It stands in a flat, about a mile from the shore, surrounded with moats indeed, but such as would prove very insignificant obstacles to an approaching enemy. Perhaps, however, it might not have been erected so much for hostile purposes as for those of state; since it appears to have been attached to a particular office, that of Constable of England, and was held by the service of the Constableship.* The antiquity of the building is uncertain; probably as high as the early Anglo Norman princes. Little of its history has reached our times, except the circumstance of its having been connected with the birth of Henry VII.[4]

---

4   The castel of Calecoyd longging to the Kinge, is in Base Venteland towardthe Severn shore, not far from Matthern. At this castel, as sum say, was King Henry VII. begotten.—Leland, *Itin.* vol. v. 5.

Leaving Caldecot, we directed our course towards Caerwent, passing through a rich, diversified country, splendidly illuminated by the beams of a glorious autumnal sun. proached this place, which is now only a miserable village, busy fancy began her magical operations, and carried us back to those times, when Caerwent flourished in all the pride of classical architecture; when, under the auspices of Agricola, its temples and theatre, porticoes and baths, almost rivalled the splendor of its maternal city; and it exhibited all the elegancies of Roman refinement. This agreeable reverie might have lasted a considerable time, had not a walk of twenty-seven miles so exhausted us, that we were soon called from "speculation high" to attend to the cravings of appetite, the loud demands of nature. Fortunately, at this moment, the sign of the Bull invited us into a snug little public-house, where we gladly seated ourselves, and quickly forgot the lords of the world, and the accomplished general of Titus, in a tankard of excellent ale, and a dish of bacon and eggs.

After satisfying our appetite, we enquired for a *ciceroni* to conduct us round the ruins of Caerwent, and to point out a famous Roman tesselated pavement, which was discovered here in July 1777. Our landlord, who appeared to be the antiquary of the place, was unfortunately prevented, by an indispensable engagement with a pipe and a pot of beer, from being our companion; he therefore committed us to the conduct of a fine lad, about eighteen, the ostler of the house, who, he assured us, and I dare say with great truth, would shew the *tiquities* just as well as himself. We had not gone far, before we observed that our guide walked very lamely, and in great apparent pain. Perceiving that it arose from his knee, which was considerably swelled, and wrapped in bandages, I inquired the nature of the injury he had received. "An please your honour," returned the boy, with a very significant look, in which fear and anger were strangely blended, "Ise got a taking." "A *taking*, my lad, what dost thou mean?" "A *witch* hard by, and be dang'd to her, has *taken* to me." We were, you may imagine, not a little surprised to discover that old popular superstition, a belief in these imaginary gifted females, existing at a place not thirty miles in a direct line from Bath. Our curiosity was awakened, and we requested the lad to give us the particulars of his misfortune. He told us, that about three weeks back, as he was working in a hedge, he suddenly found his knee extremely painful; that on examining the part he could perceive no appearance of a wound, but notwithstanding it soon swelled very much, and became considerably inflamed. On his return home, he shewed it to one of the neighbours, who very sagaciously asserted, that the injury must have been effected by supernatural means, and pointed out an old woman, the reputed witch of the village, as the invisible agent in the business. He added, he had shewn it also to his master (mine host of the Bull) who had done every thing in his power to remove the ill, by first lancing the part and afterwards burning the flesh to the bone; but that, notwithstanding these *judicious* efforts of chirurgical skill, the knee grew worse than ever; a circumstance which confirmed the patient's opinion of his being under the influence of witchery. "Well, my lad," said I, "and didst thou not go to the old lady?" "Ees, your honour, Ise went to her, but she vrighted I nationly. She lookt at 'un, zaid a vew words over un, and bade God bless me; telling me I should go home, bide quiet, pultice the knee, and be a good lad, and then I need not be afraid of her, or any other old woman. But I'll be even wi' her I war'nt, for that." The conclusion of the boy's speech rather alarmed us for the safety of the poor creature, whose age and infirmities had rendered her the object of the villagers' suspicions; but who, by the sufferer's own account, possessed more good sense and benevolence than all of them together. We therefore endeavoured to convince him, that his malady arose from natural causes; from a thorn probably in the first instance, aggravated by his master's very injudicious treatment of the afflicted part. We applauded and repeated the directions of the old lady, and prevailed, afterwards, upon the host, whom we discovered to be the village doctor, to adopt the more comfortable and simple system of rest and poultices, in the room of cauterizing and excision.

Few notices of the ancient grandeur or extent of this Roman station are now visible. Parts of the walls indeed remain, which ascertain the fortress to have been either square or oblong. These are substantial and well built; and the cement, as usual in ruins of this nature, firm, durable, and tenacious. That Caerwent, however, was of considerable importance during the Roman dominion in this country, we may conclude from the extensive ruins to be seen on the spot in Leland's time, who visited it in the beginning of the sixteenth century, and thus describes its appearance at that time:

> Cairguent in Base Venteland is iiii miles from Chepstow in the way to Caerlion. It was sum tyme a fair and a large cyte. The places where the iiii gates was yet appere, and the most part of the wal yet standith, but alto minischyd and torne. In the towne yet appere pavimentes of the old streates, and yn digging they finde fundations of great brykes, tessellata pavimenta, & numismata argentea simul & ærea.[5]

The most remarkable and curious proof of the presence of the Romans here, is a beautiful *tessellated pavement*, discovered in the year 1777, and even yet in tolerable preservation. It lies in a field belonging to a farm in the immediate neighbourhood of the village; and is twenty-four feet

---

5   *Itin.* vol. v. f. 5.

in length, and eighteen in breadth. The area consists of several compartments, containing pleasing representations of those circular involutions frequently seen in Saxon architecture, and known by the name of Runic circles. This is surrounded by a running border of an elegant pattern, in the manner of a Turkey carpet. The whole is formed of tessera or dies, nearly cubical, about three parts of a inch deep, and little more than half an inch in breadth; consisting of four colours, red, yellow, blue, and white, which are so judiciously disposed, as to give great life and spirit to the work!

You are not to be informed, my friend, that these tessellated pavements were much in request with the ancients, both in their public and private edifices. If the one we are now considering, did not form the floor of a small temple or *sacellum*, it would probably be the elegant ornament of the dwelling of some military commander, residing at this Roman station. The gentleman on whose property it was discovered, Mr. Lewis, of Chepstow, with due regard to the curiosity of this specimen of ancient art, surrounded it with a stone wall, by which means it has been in a great measure defended from injury; but still, as this inclosure is not roofed in, and as persons who visit the pavement are not prohibited from carrying away samples of the *tessera*, it is to be feared, that the violence of the elements, and the depredations of curiosity united, may in time rob the public of this curious remain.

Having spent a considerable time on the scite of the old Roman station, sighed over its perishing remains, and moralized on the transitory nature of all human grandeur, we turned into the road to Usk, and pursued our walk. A short half hour brought us to the pleasing little village of Lanvair; formerly the proud residence of some baronial chieftain, the only attestation of whose ancient splendour is the ruined shell of a castle, almost hidden from the eye by a luxuriant mantle of ivy. This hostile edifice rises immediately over the village-church, a small and lowly building, which, together with its frowning neighbour, form appropriate emblems of pride and humility, with their respective consequences. The ostentatious turrets of the castle are sunken into the dust, and "their memorial is perished with them;" whilst the lowly house of prayer, "which maketh no proud boastings," still continues to secure veneration, and attract regard. The village cemetery is bounded by the turnpike-road, and as I ever make a point of visiting any country churchyard near which I happen to pass, C—— and myself entered the consecrated ground. The well-known elegy of a favourite poet may, perhaps, have had some secret and imperceptible influence in producing this propensity; and the association of ideas may sufficiently account for a partiality towards *real* scenes, the *description* of which has afforded high gratification.

To this cause of predilection, however, may be added the reflection, which naturally arises in the mind in these repositories of the departed poor, that *here* is the conclusion of their sorrows; the happy termination of those distresses, inconveniencies, and wants, which honest experience will allow, in spite of all the fanciful reasonings of theory, the children of labour and poverty too sensibly feel.

We had soon collected the past biography of the village, from the "frail memorials" erected to commemorate the names, age, &c. of the deceased parishioners, and were leaving the church-yard, when our attention was caught by the following admonitory stanza, engraven on a stone placed as a style into it. I copied it, *verbatim et literatim*, and present it to you as a good specimen of rustic poetry and orthography:—

> Who Ever hear on Sonday
> Will Practis playing At Ball
> it Maybe beFore Monday
> The Devil will Have you all.

As it is tedious and uninteresting to walk along a turnpike-road for any considerable time, we deviated from it on leaving Lanvair, and skirted the adjoining hills and fields. From hence we were gratified with a magnificent prospect to the north and west, over a beautiful and varied country swelling into lofty elevations, and sinking into fruitful vallies, watered by a winding river, ornamented with elegant villas, and nobly bounded by the black mountains. This scene continued to Usk, which we entered about seven o'clock; and reposed ourselves at the Three-Salmons Inn, after a walk, of six and thirty miles. We were soon sufficiently refreshed by good dish of tea, to strole round the town, and visit its ruined castle, and are just returned, much pleased, from our ambulation.

The situation of Usk is very pleasing, it being built on the banks of abroad and clear river of that name. A large stone bridge is thrown over this stream to the west of the village, from whence the view, both upwards and downwards, is extremely striking. The history of Usk, you know, is in some measure connected with classical antiquity, it having been a Roman station, mentioned in the *Itinerary* of Antoninus under the name of *Burrium*. Few recent particulars respecting it are handed down to us, except that there was formerly a priory near it, (the remains of which may yet be seen) consisting of five Benedictine Nuns, founded by the St. Clare family, in the early part of the thirteenth century, and endowed with lands to the annual value of seventy pounds. The ruin also of a noble castle, standing upon a hill to the north-west of the town, makes a venerable appearance. Its origin and history, however, are buried in oblivion, and it remains a melancholy monument of the nullity of human labours; of the vanity of man's attempting to make himself a lasting name by the works of his hands.

Your's, &c.

R. W.

Letter II

TO THE SAME

DEAR SIR,   *Brecon, Aug. 15th.*

he beauty of the morning tempted us to rise at five, that we might reach Abergavenny to breakfast. This is a system, indeed, which we mean to pursue through our expedition, provided the weather encourage us to continue it; for we perfectly agree with our admirable descriptive poet, in considering the early hours of day as peculiarly calculated for the contemplation of nature, and the enjoyment of rural scenery:—

Falsely luxurious, will not man awake,
And, springing from the bed of sloth, enjoy
The cool, the fragrant, and the silent hour,
To meditation due, and sacred song?
For is there ought in sleep can charm the wise?
Who would in such a gloomy state remain
Longer than Nature craves, when every Muse,
And every blooming pleasure, wait without
To bless the wildly-devious morning walk?

Having the Usk on our left hand, we pursued its banks, as nearly as we could, without making any considerable deviation from the public way, and were gratified for our trouble by a most agreeable variety of scenery. We returned, however, to the road, about five miles from Abergavenny, in order to survey a gate-way now erecting as an entrance to the park of Clytha castle. It is an elegant piece of architecture, in the style of florid Gothic. We could not but agree, notwithstanding, that a building of greater simplicity would have been more judicious and appropriate to the other circumstances of the place. The present splendid one leads us to expect a mansion proportionately superb; and we are, therefore, not a little disappointed on entering the park, and discovering the house, to find a comfortable and substantial one indeed, but neither of dimensions nor architecture consistent with the highly-ornamented entrance through which we have just passed.

The clock told nine as we entered Abergavenny; and a walk of eleven miles rendered the excellent breakfast which we met with at the Angel inn particularly grateful. As it happened to be market-day, we had a good opportunity of observing the manners and appearance of the South-Wallians, many of whom are always collected together at this weekly meeting. We bent our course, therefore, to the *forum*, which we found thronged with people, and filled with the hum of numberless voices. In truth, it was a busy, animated, interesting scene; and to us not a little strange, from the circumstance of a language being generally spoken there, which we had not previously heard. Hitherto we had met with nothing but English; but as the markets of large Welsh towns are chiefly filled by the inhabitants of villages and hamlets from a considerable distance round, which boast neither markets nor shops, the business of the day is transacted in the language of the country. The cleanliness of the articles exposed to sale, and the neatness observable in the persons of the sellers, gave us the first favourable impression with respect to the Welsh character; for we cannot help thinking that there is generally found to be a connection between personal decency and ethical excellence, and that the effect of cleanliness extends to the morals of a man:

> E'en from the body's purity, the mind
> Receives a secret, sympathetic aid.

We were more especially pleased with the female part of the company. A round, candid, open countenance, illuminated by a brilliant complexion, dark eyes, and teeth of dazzling whiteness; and a certain indescribable *naiveté*, (which happily blends archness and simplicity, a great deal of intelligence, with an equal share of modesty) give an air peculiarly agreeable and characteristical to the Welsh girls. Some degree of whimsicality arose from our questioning these fair market-women relative to the prices of the various articles they sold, (of which we wished to acquire an accurate idea) and the difficulty that attended our being intelligible to each other. The guttural sounds they uttered, (which even the voice and manner of a Welsh girl cannot render pleasing or harmonious) were totally thrown away upon our ignorance; whilst the roughnesses and sibilisms of our own Saxon dialect, only excited an arch laugh from these virgin descendants of the ancient Britons.

You will say, we displayed but a sorry taste in leaving this fair society, to visit some fragments of antiquity; but as we had much to do in a short time, it was necessary we should quit the busy spot for a very different scene, a scene of silence and desolation-the remains of Abergavenny castle. "The thistle shakes there its lonely head; the moss whistles to the wind. The fox looks out from the windows, the rank grass of the wall waves round his head. Desolate is the dwelling of Moina, silence is in the house of her fathers."

This ruin, which was originally a Norman castle,[1] stands to the westward of the town, in such a situation as to command it compleatly, but has nothing in it striking or picturesque; no wood waving in its courts, no thickly-mantling ivy creeping round its walls. Its history is marked with infamy and treachery, and Giraldus Cambrensis records it to have been,

With many a foul and midnight murder fed;

As having been stained with more blood than any other castle of Wales. First by William son of Earl Miles, (Earl of Hereford) and afterwards by William Breos; both having upon public assurance, and under pretence of friendship, invited thither some of the Welsh nobility, and then basely murdered them.* Abergavenny itself occurs in the *Itinerary* of Antoninus, under the name of *Gobannium*, from which the present appellation is evidently derived, with the addition of the British prefix *Aber*, or harbour, and the alteration of a few letters.

---

1   Built, probably, by Hamelin Balon or Baladun, one of those who came over with the Conqueror, who also founded a priory here, towards the conclusion of the eleventh century. To this religious foundation the tithes of the castle were given in kind, *tempore Johannis*, on condition that the Abbot of St. Vincent at Mans would send overt hither a convent of Benedictine Monks. At the general suppression it was dissolved; the house consisting of a prior and four monks, and its revenues amounting to 129l. 5s. 8d. *per annum.*——Tanner's *Notitia Monastica.*

The road from this place to Crickhowel appeared very striking to us who are inhabitants of South-England, and conversant only with the comparatively tame scenery of those parts. On reaching the first elevation from Abergavenny, we turned round to contemplate the country we were passing through, which was now become mountainous, and gave us a foretaste of what we are to expect by and bye. Here we were struck with the ragged summit of Skirid Vawr, or Holy Mountain, rising to the east of the town, and the dark form of the Bloranch which lifts its proud head on the opposite side. The stupendous fissure that appears to the North of the former, gave rise to its name; tradition having impressed the belief upon the neighbouring country, that the chasm was produced at the period of our Saviour's crucifixion, when Nature herself was convulsed, and

—————————From her seat
Sighing through all her works, gave signs of woe.

As we proceeded, our progress was frequently retarded by numerous droves of black cattle from Pembrokeshire and Carmarthenshire, travelling towards the Passage, to be transported across the Severn, and driven to the markets of Bristol, and the other large towns of Somerset, Glocestershire, and Wilts. Here they are purchased by the grazier, and sent into the rich pasturage of the southern vales to be fatted, which cannot be effected in the country where they are bred. Large parties of reapers also, amounting in the whole to two or three hundred, met us on their way into Herefordshire and Glocestershire, for the harvest month; remarkable in the uniformity of their dress, which consisted of a jacket and breeches of thick striped flannel, the manufacture of the country, and dyed almost invariably of a light blue colour.

Our walk to Crickhowel was further diversified by a Druidical remain, which occurred in a field to the right hand, at the fifteenth milestone from Brecon. It is a single upright stone, thirteen or fourteen feet high, and about five over. Standing quite alone, with nothing around or near it to lead to a discovery of its original designation, we can only conjecture that it was connected with the religious worship of the ancient Britons, of whose superstition many stupendous examples of a similar nature are to be seen in almost every quarter of the kingdom.

The castle of Crickhowel led us a little out of the road, and detained us some time in examining its remains, and tracing its original plan. Wales, indeed, appears to be an admirable field for the study of ancient military architecture; as almost every considerable town, and many inconsiderable villages, exhibit their respective castles in greater or less preservation, the scene of the cumbrous magnificence and rude revelry of our forefathers, where the great lord formerly lived in princely state,

Girt with many a baron bold,

and exercising almost all the rights of sovereignty, within the precincts of his demesne. Few remains of Crickhowel castle are to be seen, many neighbouring cottages having sprung from the stones purloined from its walls.[2] They are, however, pleasingly circumstanced with ivy, and form, upon the whole, an interesting ruin. The Keep appears to have been a very secure building, seated upon a lofty artificial elevation, and displaying the foundations of a thick substantial wall.

We now reached the Beaufort Arms, the village public-house, where we refreshed ourselves with the contents of the land lady's cupboard, and a bottle of *currw*, or Welsh ale. This was the first time of our tasting the famous beverage of Wales; but I cannot say that it proved at all agreeable to our palates, though the Cambrians seek it with avidity, and quaff it with the most patient perseverance. Their ancestors, you know, displayed a similar propensity eighteen hundred years ago; and the old Celt frequently sunk un-

---

2   The castle is thought to have been abandoned after it was destroyed by Owain Glydŵr in 1403, and the stone-robbers left only the double tower on Castle Green. However, when Warner visited the ruins, the said tower was in much better condition than today, if one is to judge by 19th century illustrations. —Ed.

der the powerful influence of the ancient *currw*.[3] It was then,[4] as it is now, made from barley; but the grain is dried in a peculiar way, which gives it rather a smoky taste, and renders it glutinous, heady, and soporiferous.

As we passed on to Brecon, we observed about five miles from that town, in the hedge, on the left hand, a curious monument of the presence of the Romans in these parts. It is a sepulchral *cippus*, somewhat cylindrical, and probably about six or seven feet long, inscribed with Roman characters, rather rudely cut. Camden, I recollect, speaks of this piece of antiquity as posterior to the Roman times, for what reason I know not, and describes the inscription as follows, N—— *filius Victorini*.

Time, however, has committed such depredations upon it, that the only letters to be distinguished now, are the first half dozen of the word *Victorini*.

The exercise of walking twenty-five miles under an August sun, had rendered us exceedingly thirsty, and we looked anxiously round for a farm-house, where we might procure a draught of new milk. At length a neat little dwelling peeped out of a coppice to the right of the road, and we hastened towards it. A huge and most ferociously-looking dog, however, which rose up on our approach, and breathed a deep and threatening

---

3   *Est et Occidentis populis sua ebrietas, fruge madida.* lib. xiv.

4   *Ligures utuntur potu hordeaceo.*——Strabo, lib. iv.

growl, warned us to preserve an awful distance. We hallooed therefore at the gate of the court, in order to bring out the inhabitants of the mansion. After some time the garden wicket opened, and we saw a gigantic Welsh girl come forward, (a good companion to old *Trusty* at the door) hard as iron, and built like an Hercules, with a spade flung over her shoulder, which she had been using in the garden. We told our situation, and requested, with all the persuasions we could urge, the refreshment of which we stood so much in need. But alas! all our eloquence was thrown away; the strapping Cambrian did not understand English, and "*dym Sasna*—I know nothing of Saxon," (a term of reproach which these ancient Britons apply to us, as the creatures of yesterday) was all the answer we could get to our representation. A countryman, however, coming by at the time, we engaged him (for he fortunately spoke English) to be the interpreter between us and the damsel; and through him we again urged our request. But it was all in vain; the mistress was absent from home, and had left the mastiff and girl in charge with the house, who seemed equally true to their trust; no blandishments being of any avail in soothing the former, nor the offer of a shilling sufficient to bribe the latter, to dispose of ought that belonged to her mistress, without her knowledge and consent. Though disappointed of our expected refreshment, we could not but feel much pleased with the sturdy integrity of this domestic; and through our friend the interpreter, conveyed a trifle to her, together with a compliment on her fidelity, and a recommendation to her to continue in it. Half a mile further, however, at a place called Skethrog, our application was more successful, and we were entertained by a decent looking matron, with milk fresh from the cow, and excellent bread and butter, after refusing a tankard of cider, or a bottle of ale. As cashier, I had drawn the strings of my purse, in order to make a pecuniary return for this seasonable favour; but I was saved the trouble of offering any thing, by the positive assurance of our hostess, that she would receive no acknowledgment, "as the traveller was always welcome to any refreshment that her dwelling could afford." We had heard much of Welsh hospitality, but heard it with that degree of infidelity which ignorance is so apt to produce; it gave us therefore no little pleasure to find it exemplified towards ourselves, in an instance of such disinterested kindness as would immediately have put us into good humour with our species, had we been ever so much inclined to quarrel with it before.

We reached Brecon sufficiently early to visit the town and its environs before the close of the evening. Like most other towns in Wales, this place is interesting rather from what it has been, than on account of what it now is. During the days of chivalry and papacy, it boasted a castle and a monastery, the imperfect ruins of which still evince the former extent and grandeur of these edifices. They were both built in the reign of Henry the First, by Bernard de Newmarch, a Norman lord, who, a short time after the erection of the castle, founded near it a priory for six Benedictine Monks, and richly endowed it with lands and tithes.[5] This was a common practice with the great barons in the feudal ages, who seem to have thought that the erection of a religious house in the immediate neighbourhood of their castles, operated as an absolution for all the acts of spoliation, rapine, and misrule, exhibited within the walls of them. The castle of Brecknock passed through the families of the Braoses and Bohuns, and afterwards into that of the Duke of Buckingham, a nobleman successively the friend, favourite, enemy, and victim of Richard the Third. It was to this fortress that Moreton bishop of Ely was conveyed on his arrest by the usurper, and committed to the custody of Buckingham. The ingratitude of Richard, who, as soon as he was assured of his power, forgot the arm which had helped to vest him with it, raised the indignation of the Lord of Brecknock, and retiring to his castle, he

---

5   To the west of the town are the remains also of an ancient house of Black Monks, which Henry VIII. converted into a college, by the name of the College of Christ-church in Brecknock, and joined the college of Aberguilly to it. It now consists of the Bishop of St. David's, who presides as dean, a precentor, treasurer, chancellor, and nineteen other prebendaries. Tanner's *Not. Monast.*

there consulted with his prisoner on the means of wresting the sceptre from Richard, and returning it once more into the Lancastrian line. The plan was here digested, and eventually brought to a successful termination; though very opposite fates attended the original formers of it. Buckingham was the active engine, and shortly after the commencement of his operations, being detected and taken prisoner, he finished his restless and time-serving career on the scaffold. The bishop acted the more judicious part, he escaped from the castle, kept quiet, and lived to become, in the ensuing reign, a privy counsellor, and to fill the metropolitan see of Canterbury. Part of the castle walls and some fragments of a tower remain; the latter is said to have been the apartment in which the bishop was confined, and is still called Ely tower. Vestiges of the priory are also to be seen, and the church formerly belonging to it is now used by the parishioners for public worship. It is a large building, but I should apprehend not older than the time of Henry the Fourth. The *parvaise*, or ambulatory, where the monks were wont to walk and meditate, lies to the east of the church, and is called the Priory Walks. They have been long appropriated to the use of the inhabitants, and are wonderfully pleasant and romantic; shaded by noble trees, and watered by the loud brawling river Hondhy, which rolls at the foot of them, though so much hidden by *wood*, as only to be caught in occasional glimpses.

On returning through the church-yard, we observed, for the first time, a number of epitaphs in the language of the country; and on hearing them translated by the person who conducted us round the town, were much struck with the simplicity of their sentiment and expression. Another custom also, that was equally new to us, caught our attention; the ornamenting of graves of the deceased with various plants and flowers, at certain seasons, by the surviving relatives.[6] This last tribute of regard, this posthumous recollection, is strikingly impressive; as it speaks directly to a principle deeply rooted in the mind of man. To live in the remembrance of those we love, "when we go hence, and are no more seen," is a natural wish; a wish implanted in our souls by that Being, who willed that we should be social creatures, and gave us all the kind affections of our nature:

> For who, to dumb forgetfulness a prey,
> This pleasing anxious being e'er resign'd,
> Left the warm precincts of the pleasing day,
> Nor cast one longing, ling'ring look behind?
>
> On some fond breast the parting soul relies,
> Some pious drops the closing eye requires;

---

6   It is generally done, I understand, during the festival of Easter, the resurrection of our Saviour; and though of Pagan origin, the custom may have been appropriated by Christians to that day, to adumbrate the youth, vigour, and beauty, which the body will enjoy, "when this corruptible shall put on incorruption, and this "mortal be clothed with immortality."

E'en from the grave the voice of Nature cries:
E'en in our ashes live their wonted fires.

The practice, you know, is a very ancient one, and may be traced back as high as classical antiquity. Amongst the Greeks, (a lively and affectionate people) the decoration of the sepulchres of their deceased connections, on particular days, was observed with the most rigid punctuality; and the plants and flowers used on the occasion were not unaptly termed Ἔρωτες,[7] or the tributes of love and affection. The Romans also, who received in a great measure their religion from Greece, adopted this custom amongst other shewy and impressive superstitions; and appointed a certain season of the year when it should be more particularly observed. It was during the month of February that the solemn rites of the *feralia*, or honours paid to the manes of the departed, were performed, and the scattering of odoriferous plants and flowers upon their tombs formed one important feature of these striking ceremonies. Virgil, you may recollect, alludes to this affectionate practice in some of the finest lines of his *Æneid*; the very beautiful apostrophe to the shade of Marcellus, which so much affected the unfortunate Octavia, and produced such an handsome pecuniary reward to the poet:

---

7   Phavorin. *Etymolog.* in verb.

Heu miserande puer! si quà fata aspera rumpas,
Tu Marcellus eris. Manibus date lilia plenis:
Purpureos spargam flores, animamque nepotis
His saltem accumulem donis, et fungar inani
Munere."

Lib. vi. 882.

Our return to the inn (the Lion) was quickened by a shower of rain; and we are just preparing to discuss the events of our march, over Usk trout and Brecknockshire mutton.

Your's, &c.

R. W.

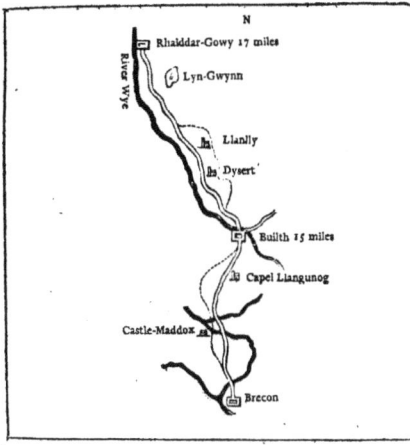

Letter III

TO THE SAME

hat a multitude of adventures may be grasped within the narrow circle of a day, by those ramblers who have spirit to investigate; curiosity to enquire; and attention to observe; who (according to the remark of a fellow-traveller) interest their hearts in every thing; and having eyes to see what time and chance are perpetually holding out to them as they journey on their way, miss nothing they can fairly lay their hands on. In a country like this, where every thing we hear, and every thing we see, is entirely new to us, you may imagine this observation is fully exemplified in ourselves. Be not surprised, therefore, should my letters savour somewhat of the prolixity of Crispinus, and the garrulity of old Ashmole, the former of whom, you know, was tedious to a proverb;[1] and the latter so minute as to favour the world with the number of his sternutations in the course of the day.[2]

As the morning was rather unfavourable, we did not leave Brecon till nine o'clock, when the clouds breaking away, and the sun appearing, we set off for Rhaiddar-Gowy, a town at the distance of thirty-two miles. The view of Brecon from the north is more agreeable and interesting than from any other point. It here appears a spacious and respectable town, climbing the declivity and brow of an eminence, with the Usk winding at its feet, and the mountain Pennervaen, rough, precipitous, and dark, rising behind it to the south. Continuing our former plan, we deviated a little from the turnpike-road, and strolled through the hay-fields, invited by their fragrance, the crop having been but lately carried in. It was not long, however, before we discovered we had wandered considerably from the road, and were perplexed

1   Hor. *Sat.* lib.i, sat. i. 120.

2   Ashmole's Life [Elias Ashmole, *Memoirs of the life of that learned antiquary, Elias Ashmole, Esq; drawn up by himself by way of diary. With an appendix of original letters* (London: Charles Burman, 1717). —Ed.]

by several tracks which crossed us in various directions. At this moment C—— observed some hay-makers in a field at no great distance; and being a Thessalian in speed, he ran to enquire the path we should pursue. Fortunately, one of the company spoke English, who, sticking his fork in the ground, and throwing on his coat and waistcoat, came to us without delay. We immediately perceived there was character in this man; a quick, dark eye, and sharp features, gave him that appearance of intellect, which is seldom found to be belied upon further acquaintance. He enquired our destination and object, and, finding us neither shy nor reserved, declared he should have a pleasure in attending us part of the road to Rhaiddar, which was somewhat difficult for strangers to trace. "But," continued he, "I cannot think of doing this, gentlemen, till you have visited my cottage hard by, and tasted my ale, of which I keep a good bottle for the refreshment of my friends." The invitation was given with so much warmth and good-will, that we accepted it without hesitation, and followed our guide to his residence. It was an humble dwelling, standing in the midst of a small but neat garden, under the side of a steep hill, sheltering it from the blasts of the east and north. On entering the tenement, which consisted only of a ground floor, we found that it was divided into two apartments; the inner one containing a bed and four chairs, the outer displaying an infinite variety of heterogeneous articles; implements of destruction, and books of divinity; culinary utensils, and apothecary's drugs; cobler's tools, and English classics; a cabinet and a cupboard, tables and stools, chairs and benches. We were shaken by the hand and bidden to sit down; when our friendly conductor, opening the cabinet, produced a bottle and glasses, the shell of a good cheese, some brown bread, and oaten cake. After the bumper of good fellowship had gone round, mine host favoured us with his history, which here counted with great spirit, and much humour, exhibiting a compleat example of that rare philosophy, which can meet the maladies of life with a smile, and rise superior to the blasts of casualty, and the frowns of fortune.

His name, he told us, was Robert Lewis, and his family one of the best in Wales. Inclination, he observed, led him to follow a profession, but his friends thinking a trade likely to prove more advantageous, he was bound apprentice to a tanner. Happily or unfortunately, for he was doubtful in which light to consider it, a fair damsel (the daughter of a neighbouring hidalgo, who had more than an usual portion of national pride) beheld him with complacency; and the regard being mutual, he eluded the vigilance of her parents, bore her off to a neighbouring church, and made her his wife. The idea of their fair relation being matched with a man in trade, was what her haughty kinsmen could not brook; the father's pride more especially was sorely wound-

ed, and the whole clan vowed to revenge the af-
front. Their first attempts were of a very hostile
nature, and Lewis recounted a number of "hair-
breadth 'scapes," and "most disastrous chances,"
which he had experienced from their malice; being frequently shot at from ambuscades, or encountered at night on returning to his dwelling.
None of these adventures, however, terminated
fatally to him, the aggressors in general coming
off the worse, he being a man of great vigour, ac-
tivity, and spirit. Finding their expectations disappointed, therefore, his enemies changed their
plan of operations, and since they could not injure his person, they determined to destroy his
fortune. Here they were at length successful, as
art and cunning will ever be when opposed to
candour and incaution. By a long series of ma-
licious schemes, they ruined his business, blast-
ed his credit, and drove him from the country
where he was settled. "All this, however, gentlemen," continued he, "hard as it may seem, I
could have borne with patience, had the effects of
their vengeance extended no further. But, alas!
they wounded me in a tenderer part, they robbed
me of my Letty! she died of a broken heart, and
left me a widower, with four children. I confess,
I had much difficulty in bearing up against this
blow, and I was on the point of sinking into de-
spair. A short time, however, and a little reflection, brought me to myself; I recollected that the
partner of my heart was now much happier than

I could have made her; that she had left me many duties to perform; and that, in proportion to my difficulties and distresses, should be my exertion and endeavours to remove them. I therefore arranged my affairs, got into a smaller line of business, brought up my children, and sent them into the world. Having done this, and saved a trifle for a rainy day, I left the busy haunts of men, and purchased the cottage in which you now are; where I experience as much happiness as I can hope for on this side of the grave. My children, I bless GOD! all turned out well, and are decently provided for; my health is sound; my mind calm and serene; 'tis true I have but little; my wants, however, are proportioned to my means, and whilst I have wherewith to procure a crust and a bottle of ale for the refreshment of a friend, I care not who possesses the riches and luxuries of life. In short," said he, "I cannot express my sentiments and situation better than in the words of the poet;" and, snatching a book that lay by him, he read, with great spirit, the following copy of verses from Percy's *Ancient English Poetry*, his eye glistening all the while with the consciousness of independence, and seeming to say,

> How vain the ardour of the croud!
> How *low*, how *indigent* the proud!
> How *little* are the *great!*
>
> My minde to me a kingdome is;
> Such perfect joye therein I finde,

As farre exceeds all earthly blisse,
  That GOD or Nature hath assignde:
Though much I want what most would have,
Yet still my mind forbids to crave.

Content I live, this is my stay;
  I seek no more than may suffice:
I presse to bear no haughtie sway;
  Look what I lack my mind supplies.
Loe! thus I triumph like a king,
Content with that my minde doth bring.

I see how plentie surfets oft,
  And hastie clymbers soonest fall:
I see that such as sit aloft
  Mishap doth threaten most of all;
These get with toile, and keep with feare:
Such cares my minde could never beare.

No princely pompe, nor welthie store,
  No force to winne the victorie,
No wylie wit to salve a sore,
  No shape to winne a lover's eye;
To none of these I yield as thrall,
For why? my mind dispiseth all.

Some have too much, yet still they crave,
  I little have, yet seeke no more;
They are but poore, though much they have;
  And I am rich with little store:
They poor, I rich; they beg, I give;
They lacke, I lend; they pine, I live.

I laugh not at another's loss,
  I grudge not at another's gaine;
No worldly wave my minde can tosse,
  I brooke that is another's bane:

I feare no foe, nor fawne on friend;
I loth not life, nor dread mine end.

My welth is helth, and perfect ease;
  My conscience clear my chiefe defence;
I never seeke by brybes to please,
  Nor by desert to give offence;
Thus do I live, thus will I die;
Would all did so as well as I.

It was with difficulty we prevailed on our hospitable host to allow us to pursue our journey, after having finished the third bottle of his *quadrimum*. He insisted, however, on being our companion for a few miles, and putting us into the direct road to Bualt. When the period of separation arrived, he grasped us by the hand, and bid us heartily farewell, adding this parting benediction:— "God bless you! gentlemen, and may your journey through life be as pleasant as your walk is likely to prove. But should storms and difficulties await you, remember that a clear conscience, an independent spirit, and a reliance on Providence, will enable you to brave them all, and bring you happily home at the last."

Our attention was not particularly awakened by any circumstance till within a mile of Bualt, when we passed (on the turnpike-road) a bridge thrown over a mountain brook, the scenery around which is very striking; a rent or fissure of the mountain, formed probably by some natural convulsion, opens to the left, through which a torrent throws itself over a bed of stones. The sides of the chine are rocky and abrupt, but finely softened and relieved by trees of various sorts, which are sprinkled over the face of the rock, and descending many spots quite to the edge of the stream. It was on the banks of this river, but further to the northward, that the decisive battle was fought between the gallant Llewellyn, the last prince of Wales, and the forces of Edward the First. The Cambrian chieftain, it seems, was not present at the commencement of the action, which other ways might have terminated favourably for him. Edmund Mortimer and John Gifford the English commanders, understanding that Llewellyn had retired from his host, in order to confer with the Radnorshire chieftains, led their men to the attack, and the first notice of the event which reached the Prince's ear, was brought to him by his own flying troops. All that a brave leader, and an experienced soldier, could effect in such a situation, Llewellyn performed; he rallied his men, led them again to the conflict, and animated them by his own example. Fate, however, had decreed that his efforts should be ineffectual; his army was entirely routed, and the spear of Adam de Francton pierced his heart whilst he was performing prodigies of valour, and happily prevented him from surviving the lost liberties of his country. The body of the Prince, covered with honourable wounds, was discovered, and dispatched to Edward at Conway, who received it with a savage joy. After having sated his fury by offering many marks of ignominy to the lifeless remains, he sent them to London, where the citizens exceeded even their monarch in brutality, exhibiting an instance of that ferocity and want of feeling with which a system of war is found to stain a national character. They carried it through Cheapside upon the point of a lance, decorated with a silver crown; then placed it in the common pillory, and afterwards exposed it on the highest part of the tower of London. "Such a barbarous triumph over the body of a brave prince, (as the historian properly observes) who died in the defence of it being in Brecknockshire, and the other in Radnorshire. Leaving this on our left, we pursued the road to Rhaiddar, which runs over the hill to the eastward of the river. We had not proceeded more than a mile, before the scenery of the Wye became too interesting to be passed with transient observation; we therefore threw ourselves on its eastern bank under the shade of a friendly aspin tree, to contemplate its beauties at leisure. At this spot the view is particularly striking. The river appears at our feet, dashing and roaring through a bed of huge, misshapen rocks, and forming, in its struggles, numberless whirlpools, eddies, and small cascades. A bank, rude, abrupt, and bare, rises before us, pleasingly contrasted by the verdant and wooded declivity opposite to it. As the eye roves up the river, it catches softer beauties; the sides become less precipitous, and more thickly clothed with trees. The woods at length descend to the brink of the stream, which, making a quick turn at the distance of a mile, is suddenly lost in a deep mass of shade. The back ground is formed by the mountains of Montgomeryshire, whose lofty summits rise into the clouds, and give a magnificent finishing to the scene. It was not without regret that we quitted this spot to pursue our walk, admonished by the consideration of our having sixteen miles further to go, and the sun being within two hours of "the place of his rest." In truth, we soon discovered that we had already been too dilatory; the day beginning to close, attended with no very agreeable circumstances. It was an evening of Ossian; and the scenery around rendered his description very appropriate. "Autumn is dark on the mountains; grey mist rests on the hills. The whirlwind is heard on the heath. Dark rolls the river through the narrow plain." In proportion as the light of day faded from us, the roads became more rocky, unequal, and abominable. A considerable quantity of rain had fallen a few hours before, which filling up the numberless inequalities with which these stony ways abound, we continually plunged into pools of mud, and stumbled over rocky fragments, alternately hazarding the pains of suffocation, and the fracture of our limbs. This very agreeable amusement continued till half past nine o'clock, when we were blessed with the sight of a rush-light glimmering through

the window of the Angel inn, which we entered
about two hours ago. Our first appearance was
made in the kitchen, where a scene was exhibited
that would have afforded an admirable subject
for the pencil of Hogarth. A large table covered
with rounds of beef, loins of pork, fragments of
geese, &c. &c. appeared at one end, round which
was seated a motley groupe of noisy Welsh rus-
tics, who voraciously devoured the good things
before them. Opposite to these were two Scotch
pedlars, eating their frugal repast in silence, an
oaten cake, and rock-like cheese, and diluting it
with "acid tiff;" their eyes rivetted in wistful gaze,
on the substantial fare which smoked on the adjoining table. The middle of the kitchen was occupied by a number of sportsmen just returned
from growse shooting on the mountains, cleaning their guns, and preparing them for the mor-
row's amusement. In the background flamed an
enormous fire, where a counterpart of dame Leo-
narda was preparing another set of joints, for a
second party of sportsmen who were just arrived.
Tired pointers and snoring spaniels were scattered over the floor, and completed the picture.
Notwithstanding the disadvantageous figure we
made, (for to confess the truth we were marvel-
lously foul) and the numerous guests who called
on the mistress of the house in all directions, we
met with an attention and civility from Mrs. Evans (the hostess) that will always claim our grateful remembrance. We were shewn into a snug lit-

tle room, and speedily regaled with a sumptuous supper. To check, however, in some measure, the pleasure which arose from the comparison of our present situation with what we had experienced in the last six miles of our walk, we were given to understand, that only one of us could be accommodated with a bed in the house, and that the other must sleep at a cottage a quarter of a mile distant from it. Sad news this, to tired travellers, on a stormy night! Something, notwithstanding, was to be done, and one of us must brave the pelting of a pitiless storm that rattled against the casements.—*Jacta sit alea.*—We determined to toss up for the chamber at the Lion, and fortune has just declared in favour of C———. I am not apt to grieve at the success of another, but I confess I never felt more inclined to quarrel with the fickle goddess for her decision, than on the present occasion, when a long walk through execrable roads has almost deprived me of the faculty of loco-motion.

Your's, &c.

R. W.

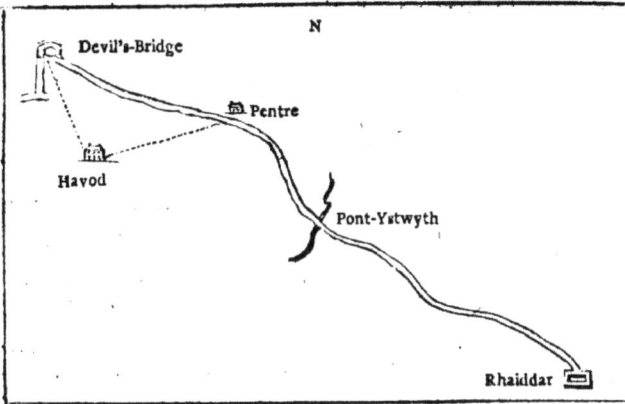

Letter IV

TO THE SAME

DEAR SIR,   *Devil's Bridge, Aug. 17th.*

his has been a day of beauties, wonders, and horrors; and though including the shortest walk we have hitherto taken, has exhibited a greater variety of extraordinary and impressive scenery, than we have witnessed since our departure from Bath. At eight o'clock we had finished our breakfast, paid our very reasonable bill, and quitted the town of Rhaiddar.[1] Our road

---

1   In enquiring for this place it is necessary for the traveller to pronounce it Rhaithar, as, in Welsh, the double d has the

first conducted us over a modern stone bridge of one arch, which bestrides the Wye to the north-west of the town. Here the river again displays much of that impetuosity which we had before observed in it, foaming over its adamantine bed, and forming a cascade of several feet almost immediately under the bridge. The foot-path winds by its margin through the meadows, leaving the turnpike-road a few hundred yards to the right. We continued along the banks of the Wye about a mile, and then ascended the mountains which run parallel with it, that we might command the view of the vale we had been passing through. It was, in truth, a pleasing, varied landscape. The sinuous course of the river; the vivid verdure of the meadows which it waters; the little town of Rhaiddar, with its neat white-washed cottages; and the dark mountains which surround it on every side, combined to produce a picture new and striking. Descending again into the road we pursued its undulations; sometimes hanging upon the brow of a lofty mountain of schistus; at other times winding under beetling precipices of rude rock, whose black projecting masses seemed to threaten destruction to the passing traveller. Every thing is in unison with this description. The waving woods, which had beautified our former prospects, now disappeared. The neat cottages, which had hitherto ornamented the vallies, now ceased to enliven the scene. Man had fled "the

---

force of the English th.

dismal situation waste and wild;" and no traces of human society appeared, except in two or three small hovels, which occurred in the course of ten miles, and were inhabited by the joyless beings who tended the widely-spread flocks that fed upon these mountains. This desolate picture was at length relieved by a little hamlet, upon which the road suddenly turns, about eleven miles from Rhaiddar. Here the river Ystwyth, with a fury very disproportionate to its size, rushes under a handsome stone bridge, built by Mr. Baldwin, of Bath, in 1783, at the expence of Colonel Johnes, of Hafôd; the finished architecture of which is contrasted by the irregular disposition of numberless misshapen rocks, which form the sides and bed of this roaring stream. While we were admiring the romantic beauties of the spot, our attention was attracted by an angler throwing his line for trout and salmon-peal, with which the rivers of Wales abound. The curious circumstance attending this sportsman was his using the left hand only in his operations, and managing, under that apparent disadvantage, a line of uncommon length. On addressing some enquiries to him, we found he had formerly been engaged in working a lead mine, but having had his right arm crushed when blasting a rock, he was obliged to relinquish that employment; and had now recourse to fishing, for the support of himself and family, in which he was very successful, being able with his left arm to throw a line of twenty-two yards in length. Finding him a shrewd intelligent fellow, and knowing there were some lead mines in the neighbourhood, we requested him to accompany us thither. This he readily assented to, and in a quarter of an hour conducted us to the spot. These subterraneous excavations lie in the side of the mountains which rise to the right of the river, and are called Cwm-yr-ystwyth[2] mines. The proprietor is a gentleman of Aber-ystwyth, whose profits from them amounted annually in times of peace to seven thousand pounds; war, however, slackening the demand for the article, and interrupting the markets, has diminished his receipts considerably, and they produce at present little more than half as much. Its evils extend also to the labourer, who, instead of six guineas, (the wages he received during peace) now clears only five guineas per ton. For this sum he bores for the vein, blasts the rock, extracts, cleans, and sorts the ore, and produces one ton of it fit for the furnace. The miner's employment is laborious, and dangerous; and his profits uncertain. Frequent injuries happen to him in blasting the rock, and digging the ore; and cold, damp, and vapour, unite in destroying his health, and shortening his life. As his gains are hardly earned, they are also precarious. Being paid not according to the quantum of his labour, but in proportion to the measure of marketable

---

2   The letter w has, in Welsh, the same pronunciation as the oo in English; this word should consequently be pronounced Coom.

ore which he produces, it frequently happens that two or three weeks elapse without his collecting a sufficient quantity to pay the expence of his gunpowder and candles. In these cases the master advances a money to the miner, sufficient for the sum of support of his family, which he returns when fortune has directed him to a rich vein of ore. It is now that he makes up for his antecedent ill-luck, and one, and even two guineas have been the rich reward of every day's labour for three or four successive weeks. Nothing in deed can better illustrate the uncertainty of a miner's profits than a circumstance told us by one of them: that he was sometimes in arrear to his master fifteen or twenty guineas for monies advanced to him, which he had been able to liquidate in ten days or a fortnight, and provide for his family at the same time, by the fortunate discovery of a productive vein. This success, however, is not so frequent as to keep the labourer above extreme poverty; nor does his gain appear to be at all equal to the toil, danger, and ill effects, of his painful avocation, which he pursues with unremitting exertion for eight hours everyday, from six o'clock till two. The laborious process of digging for the level, blasting the rock, extracting the ore, and reducing it into small masses, is performed by the men; the less toilsome task of sifting, washing, and cleaning it, is left to their wives and children. The whole operation is short and simple. When the ore is extracted and brought to a particular spot, the first employment of the workman is to beat it into small lumps, with a heavy hammer. It is then separated from the quartz, spar, and other substances connected with it, in its natural state. These masses are again reduced to a smaller size, by similar means, and afterwards thoroughly sifted, washed, and cleansed from every impurity. The next step is its removal to the stamping mill, where it is cast into a large wooden trough, and pounded into small particles, the size of a pin's head, by heavy beams of timber, shod with massive iron weights. These beams are made of oak or some other ponderous wood, several feet in length; they are elevated and depressed by means of a water-mill, and discharged with mighty force on the matter to be granulated. The ore, by this process being sufficiently pulverized, is conveyed into a trench, thro' which a certain quantity of water gently flows; here it subsides, and settles at the bottom, whilst the remaining impurities are carried off by the stream. The article is then marketable, and sent away for exportation. Lead is found in two mountains contiguous to each other; but the product of that nearest to Rhaiddar is said to be the more valuable. It is also acquired with the greater ease, the levels being driven not more than twenty or thirty yards into the mountain; whilst the other is penetrated to the prodigious extent of three hundred yards.

A neighbouring house of entertainment afforded us an opportunity of returning the fisher man's civility, by treating him with a bottle of his favourite *currw*. Our gratitude produced additional favours, and he insisted on conducting us round the walks of Hafôd, through which we might pass in our way to the Devil's-Bridge, by a route not very circuitous. A short distance therefore from the village of Pentré, we turned down a lane to the left, and soon found ourselves in the romantic scenery of Colonel Johnes's[3] celebrated place. In order to form a faint idea of this spot, you must, my dear sir, picture to yourself a deep and narrow valley, winding between mountains of towering height and fantastic shapes, thickly mantled with luxuriant woods, which fringe the precipitous sides of these enormous protuberances from their summits to their base. Through this valley, the river Ystwyth, a truly alpine stream, impetuous, foaming, and fierce, throws its crystalline waters; sometimes darting from an open rocky ledge into a deep and dark abyss below; at others, pouring through the gloomy recesses of an impenetrable wood, and discovering its course only by the roaring of its waters; increasing its current as it flows, by the addition of numberless little streams, which leaping down the mountains in all directions, hurry to unite themselves with it. On a gentle rise of land, which swells gradually from the river, and backed by a noble wood, that shelters it from the eastern blasts, stands the delightful mansion of Mr. Johnes, built in

---

3   The present Member of Parliament for Cardiganshire.

the modern Gothic style, uniting every possible convenience and comfort with an appearance of the greatest elegance, and the most correct taste.[4] Around it are walks varied and extensive, commanding views beautiful, romantic, and astonishing; woods and rocks; bridges and cataracts; the highly-ornamented garden, and the rude, rugged, uncultivated mountain. Indeed, the whole together forms a scene so striking, that while wandering through its ever-changing beauties, we feel no inclination to tax Mr. Cumberland with enthusiasm, when he declared, that in ten years travelling through the Alps, the Apennines, the Sabine Hills, and the Tyrolese; the shores of the Adriatic; the Glaciers of Switzerland; and the banks of the Rhine; he never saw anything so fine, never so many pictures concentered in one spot. It is no small addition to the pleasure we experienced in contemplating the wonders of this delicious retreat, to reflect that its enlightened and liberal owner is alive to its beauties, and enjoys the scenes which his own elegant taste has contributed to render perfect.

> Happy the man who to these shades retires,
> Whom Nature charms, and whom the Muse inspires;

---

4   The version of Hafod House seen by Warner had been completed in 1785, replacing the earlier, Tudor structure. It was destroyed by a fire in 1807 and rebuilt by Thomas Baldwin, who completed the project in 1810. The estate went into decline in the early 20th century, however, and the house was abandoned in 1942, only to be demolished in 1956. —Ed.

Whom humbler joys of home felt quiet please,
Successive study, exercise, and ease.

Here it is that Mr. Johnes, in the bosom of an united family, and in the rational society of estimable friends, passes all those hours, which his public duties do not lay claim to; relieving poverty, encouraging industry, diffusing happiness, and affording a noble example of that active benevolence, which, if it always accompanied the power of doing good, would be found to be the surest guardian of extensive possessions, as well as the greatest blessing which their enjoyment can bestow.

I assure you it was not without an effort that we left the scenery of Hafôd, after having exhausted three hours in surveying only a part of its beauties; admonished, however, by the approach of evening, we turned our faces towards the Devil's-Bridge, and wound up a steep ascent to gain the road which led thither. For a considerable distance the country formed a striking contrast to that which we had just quitted. It was barren, dull, and uninteresting, with nothing to vary the scene, but a few straggling sheep, which brouzed the scanty herbage of the hills. We continued gradually ascending for nearly three miles, when we reached an elevation that recompensed us in a moment for the severe toil of an hour. Immediately below us lay the truly astonishing and tremendous scenery of the neighbourhood of the Devil's Bridge. A profound chasm, stretching nearly east and west for upwards of a mile, the almost perpendicular sides of which are compleatly covered with trees of different kinds; the elegant foliage of the mountain ash, the mournful shade of the pensile birch, and the broad arms of the majestic oak. Through the bottom of this abyss the river Mynach pours its roaring tide, hidden from the eye by the deep shade of surrounding woods, but bursting upon the ear in the awful "sound of many waters;" in the thunder of numerous cataracts, leaping from ledge to ledge, and lashing the hollows of excavated rocks, which reverberate and multiply the roar. Immediately above this rich but awful scene, rise the neighbouring hills of Cardiganshire, bleak, barren, and dark, assuming the most fantastic shapes, and thrown about in the wildest confusion. The horizon is bounded by the lofty summits of the more important mountains of Montgomeryshire and Merioneth, amongst which the broad, huge head of Plimhimmon exalts itself to the skies. We descended the hill, and proceeded to the Hafod Arms, a neat and comfortable house, built by Mr. Johnes, one amongst other instances of his public spirit, as it was erected for the accommodation of those who visit the wonders of this singular country.[5] We were for some time in painful suspence whether or not we could procure beds for the night, as the house is full, and the apartments

---

5   The building later burnt down and was rebuilt, with significant renovations being completed in 1837 - 1839 and in the 1860s. —Ed.

all occupied; at length, however, we were made easy by the information that a neighbouring gentleman would accommodate us at his villa, which stands about half a mile from the inn. Having ordered refreshment for our friendly conductor, and *surprised* him by a small gratuity (for he exhibited another instance of Welsh disinterested kindness) C——— and I proceeded to explore the horrors of the Devil's-Bridge by ourselves, the guide (who is the master of the house) being absent from home. Our first observations were made from the bridge. This consists of a single arch, nine and twenty feet in the span, thrown over the original one (which still remains) in the year 1753.[6] The chasm that yawns under these arches is so overhung by wood, that the eye with difficulty catches even a partial view of the gloomy abyss below. This circumstance, however, heightens the impressions of terror, which such a scene is calculated to inspire. Fancy, free, and fond of painting for herself, pourtrays with her magic pencil to the mind, wonders that exceed reality; horrors which have no "local habitation," and exist only in the vivid and ever-shifting pictures of the imagination. In order to obtain a nearer and less interrupted view of this tremendous fissure, and the torrent that rush-

---

6   The old arch was built by the Monks of *Strata Florida* Abbey (a religious house ten miles from hence, the picturesque ruins of which still remain) about the conclusion of the eleventh century. It is called in Welsh *Pont-ar-Mynach*, the bridge of the Mynach; and *Pont-ar-Diawl*, the bridge of the Devil; vulgar superstition asserting Satan to be the constructor of it.

es through it, we proceeded over the bridge; and turning quickly round to the right hand, descended an abrupt and perilous path that conducted us to the base of the rocks on the eastern side of the arch. Language is but ill calculated to convey an accurate idea of the scene which is here presented to the eye. The awful height of the fissure, which the bridge bestrides one hundred and twenty feet above the observer, rendered doubly gloomy by its narrowness, and the wood which overhangs it; the stunning noise of the torrent thundering at his feet, and struggling through black, opposing rocks, which its ceaseless impetuosity has worn into shapes strange and grotesque; fill the mind with a mingled but sublime emotion of astonishment, terror, and delight. Having gratified our curiosity here, we clambered up the perpendicular path, and going in a left hand direction from the bridge, about two hundred yards, pursued a winding descent that leads to a rocky projection, which commands a view of the noble cataracts to the westward of the arch. Here the Mynach, bursting at once upon the eye in all its terrific majesty, is seen throwing itself down ragged rocks at least two hundred and ten feet, in four separate, tremendous falls. The first is a leap of nearly twenty feet; after which it is received by a fathomless bason, where for a moment it seems to rest its turbid waters, in order to recruit its strength and pour with greater violence down a second fall of sixty feet. Its third attempt decreases again to twenty feet, and here it falls amongst broken rocks, which in vain present themselves as barriers to its passage. This opposition gives it tenfold rage, and rushing over a projecting ledge with wonderful velocity, it tumbles headlong down a descent of one hundred and ten feet, and then hurries through a stony channel to unite its waters with the Rhiddol, which rushes from the opposite mountains with nearly similar grandeur and impetuosity. We should have protracted our contemplations amid this awful scenery for some time, had not a sudden flash of lightning and a loud clap of thunder, issuing from a black cloud that had imperceptibly gathered round our heads, warned us to seek the friendly shelter of our inn. We accordingly ascended the steep side of the dale, gathering in our way the *Rubus Idæus* and *Vaccinium uliginosum*, and hastened to the Hafôd Arms, at which we arrived just time enough to avoid the "mingled storm" that rages without doors, where, even now, in the language of Thomson,

Huge Uproar lords it wide.

Your's, &c.

R. W.

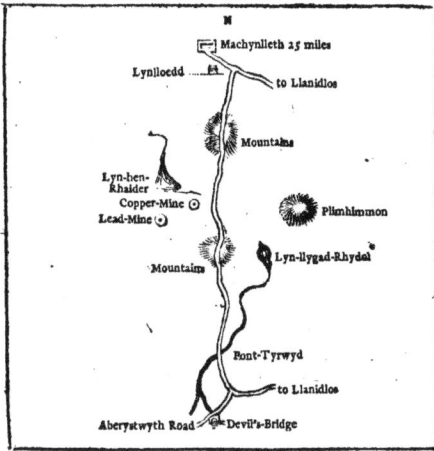

Machynlleth 25 miles

Lynllocdd

to Llanidlos

Mountains

Lyn-hen-Rhaider
Copper-Mine ⊙
Lead-Mine ⊙

Plinlimmon

Mountains

Lyn-llygad-Rhydal

Pont-Tyrwyd

to Llanidlos

Aberystwyth Road

Devil's-Bridge

Letter V

TO THE SAME

DEAR SIR, *Devil's Bridge, Friday Morning, Nine o'Clock.*

I could almost say with the unfortunate Clarence,

O, I have pass'd a miserable night,
So full of fearful sounds, of ugly sights,
That as I am a Christian faithful man,
I would not spend another such a night,
Though 'twere to buy a world of happy days;
So full of dismal terror was the time.

I have already observed to you, that as the rooms

of the inn had all been engaged before our arrival, C—— and I were obliged to sleep at a house some distance from it, the only private one in this wild and solitary neighbourhood. Flattering ourselves that the tempest would decrease, we passed the time till the clock told ten, very agreeably, at our comfortable quarters, in the company of a gentleman and two ladies, who obligingly invited us to share their sitting room, and join their party. Finding, however, that the storm rather increased than abated, we determined to brave its fury, and seek our lodging. We therefore prevailed upon a postillion to accompany us, and the terrified chambermaid who carried linen for our beds; and, thus conducted, commenced our expedition. But never shall I forget the sublimity of the scene which presented itself to us when we reached the Devil's-Bridge. The winds seemed to blow, with all their rage, from all their quarters. The thunder rattled through the sky in peals, loud, successive, and almost uninterrupted. The cataracts which tumbled beneath us, strengthened by the accumulation of waters produced by a torrent of rain, added to the din by their ceaseless, aggravated roar; whilst the lightning bursting occasionally from the pitchy mantle which curtained the whole hemisphere, at one moment displayed all the gloomy horrors of the scenery around us, and in the next left us involved in impenetrable darkness. It was the tempest described by the poet; and the circumstances of the neighbouring country were happily appropriate to his description:—

>   . . . . Wide-rent, the clouds
> Pour a whole flood: and yet, its flame unquench'd,
> Th' unconquerable lightning struggles through
> Ragged and fierce, or in red whirling balls,
> And fires the mountains with redoubled rage.
> . . . . The gloomy woods
> Start at the flash, and from their deep recess
> Wide-flaming out, their trembling inmates shake.
> Amid Carnarvon's mountains rages loud
> The repercussive roar: with mighty crash
> Into the flashing deep, from the rude rocks
> Of Penmaenmaur, heap'd hideous to the sky,
> Tumble the smitten cliffs; and Snowdon's peak
> Dissolving, instant yields his wintry load.
> Far-seen the heights of heathy Cheviot blaze,
> And Thulé bellows through her utmost isles.

It was not without difficulty and danger that we reached our destination: the violence of the wind impeding our progress, and the chasm which we skirted, hidden by the surrounding gloom, rendering every step perilous. On our arrival at the mansion (which was nothing more than a large farm-house) we were received by a stout Welsh female, who conducted us in silence, for she could speak no English, through a long passage, to our respective apartments. The first defect that I discovered in mine, was the want of shutters and curtains to exclude the vivid lightning which darted through the window every minute. I threw myself, notwithstanding, into bed, and fell immediately asleep. My mind, however, had been so struck by the terrific scenery of the day, and the awful circumstances of the night, that the impressions which they had excited still remained strongly marked upon it; and fancy, (according to the philosophy of the poet)[1] taking advantage of the hour when reason reposes herself, conjured up ten thousand horrible shapes;

> All monstrous, all prodigious things,
> Abominable, unutterable, and worse,
> Than fables yet have feign'd, or fear conceiv'd,
> Gorgons, and Hydras, and Chimeras dire.

In short, my friend, I woke in the horrors, just time enough to observe, by the glare of a flash of lightning, an object, black and huge, glide softly out of my room.

---

[1] But know that in the soul
Are many lesser faculties, that serve
Reason as chief; among these Fancy next
Her office holds; of all external things,
Which the five watchful senses represent,
She forms imaginations, airy shapes,
Which Reason joining or disjoining, frames
All what we affirm, or what deny, and call
Our knowledge or opinion; then retires
Into her private cell when nature rests.
Of tin her absence mimic Fancy wakes
To imitate her; but misjoining shapes,
Wild works produces oft, and most in dreams,
Ill matching words and deeds long past or late.
MILTON's *Par. Lost.*

Obstupui, steteruntque comæ, et vox faucibus hæsit.

Almost at the same moment several deep groans, which seemed to proceed from the adjoining passage, reached my ear. I honestly confess I am no hero, and therefore felt a considerable degree of alarm, though I did not know exactly what to fear. I started out of bed, however, and grasping my faithful oaken staff, sallied into the passage, with a view of communicating to C—— what I had seen and heard. But before I proceeded three steps without the door, my nose encountered some hard projecting substance so violently, as nearly to level me with the floor. Corporal anguish quickly banished mental alarm; I returned to my room, and barricading the entrance with a table and chair, (for there was no latch or fastning) crept again into bed, where, after a time, sleep once more wrapt me in forgetfulness. Morning developed the mystery of the apparition and noise; a large, black sheep-dog, which I saw upon the stairs, accounting sufficiently for the one; and a patient in a violent paroxysm of the tooth-ache, explaining the cause of the other.

On our return to the inn we again visited the scenery of the Devil's-Bridge, which had received additional grandeur from the deluges of the night. The view of the falls was less distinct, and consequently more sublime, than on the preceding day; a mist floated over the abyss, arising from the foaming troubled waters below, which prevented us from seeing the cataracts in detail, and gave to the eye one unbroken whole of dreadful majesty. Upon this cloud of vapour, the sun, occasionally bursting out, threw its light; and the rays being refracted from the spherical drops which composed it, produced the effect of a vivid rainbow, and added inexpressible beauty to the scene.

The attentive and obliging host has just provided us with our excellent breakfast; and when we have dispatched it, we shall cross the mountains to Machynlleth, where I purpose to finish my present epistle.

***

Machynlleth,[2] *8 o'clock Friday Evening.*

We have at length completed a tiresome walk of twenty-five miles, over mountains bleak, barren, and boggy, enlivened with few objects to interest or delight. Having engaged a guide to accompany us, we left the Hafôd Arms about ten o'clock, and pursued (what the Welsh affect to call) the turnpike to Llanidlos for a mile and half. Here a bridle-road branches off, to the left, by which we descend to a small hamlet

2   This place is pronounced *Mahunkleth*, the *c* dropping its Dower, the *y* assuming the sound of *u*, and the double having the force of *chl* or *hl*.

called Pont-ar-wyd, or wide bridge, from an accommodation of that kind thrown over the river Ryddol. During this short distance we were
amused by numberless cataracts, pouring from
the mountains in all directions, occasioned by
the copious rains of the night, which we had
been deprecating from the first moment they
fell; but without which, half the beauty of this
mountainous scenery would have been lost to
us; so true is it, that by those who are inclined to
search for the good contained in apparent evil,
every inconvenience will be found to be attended by its commensurate advantage. Ten miles
from the Devil's-Bridge, we passed the foot of
"huge Plimhimmon" the fruitful father of rivers,
from whose "cloud-capt head" flow the vagarious Wye, and noble Severn, with other less important streams. There is nothing either picturesque or fantastic in the form of this mountain;
but, rising with dignity above the neighbouring
elevations, it conveys the idea of massy solidity,
and substantial majesty. Our guide now conducted us by the side of two large lead-mines,
and a copper-mine, where we saw the process
of extracting, cleansing, stamping, and dressing
the ore, performed in a manner similar to what I
have observed in a former letter. At a short distance from this spot, after climbing a steep hill,
we were suddenly surprised with a magnificent
mountain scene. The jagged head of Cader-Idris, and the solitary summit of Snowdon, make

conspicuous figures in the picture, which is rendered compleat in its kind by the "thousand subject hills" of all shapes and forms that rise around them. This noble prospect was but of short duration; we soon descended into a boggy bottom, that continued till within three miles of Machynlleth, when a rugged carriage-road received, and conducted us into the town. The situation of this place is extremely pleasing, watered by the broad and crystalline Dovy; surrounded by verdant meadows, and sheltered from the winds by lofty mountains on every side. In this sequestered spot did the great Welsh hero, Owen Glendower, assemble the States of the Principality in 1402, and accept from their hands the crown of Wales, of which his first successes seemed to promise him the eventual possession. His career, however, had nearly been checked in an early stage, by the treachery of Sir David Gam, the mortal enemy of Owen, who intended to murder him whilst conferring with his chieftains in the parliament of Machynlleth. Fortunately, the design was detected, and Glendower, contrary to the spirit and practice of the times, had the generosity and fortitude to forgive the traitor. We have been shewn the old, barn-like house, in which this memorable synod was convened, by an attendant at our inn, (the Wynne Arms) who, as we approached it, gradually warmed into an enthusiastic strain of eulogy on the character of the old warrior.

The persuasion of portents having attended his birth, and of his being a proficient in the art of magic, had been impressed upon the mind of our guide by tradition, and his absurd stories brought to our recollection that description of himself which the muse of Shakespeare has put into the mouth of Owen:—

> . . . . At my nativity,
> The front of Heaven was full of fiery shapes,
> Of burning cressets; and, at my birth,
> The frame and the foundation of the earth
> Shak'd like a coward.——
> ——I can call spirits from the vasty deep,
> And teach thee, cousin, to command the devil.

Favoured and protected by Richard the Second, to whom he had been squire of the body, Owen continued the firm friend of this unfortunate monarch to the termination of his miseries; and having been contumeliously treated by Richard's sucessor, he boldly took arms, and laid claim to the crown of Wales, as lineal descendant of the great Llewellyn. For fifteen years did he pursue his claim with various success, in opposition to all the efforts of Henry the Fourth, and his war-like son; at length, however, death put a period to his hopes and fears, at the house of his daughter on the 20th of September, 1415, in the sixty-first year of his age. The generous attempt of Owen was not indeed crowned with success, but his name still lives in the recollection of his grateful

countrymen, who venerate him as the last asser-
tor of their liberties, the last hero of Cambria,

Your's, &c.

R. W.

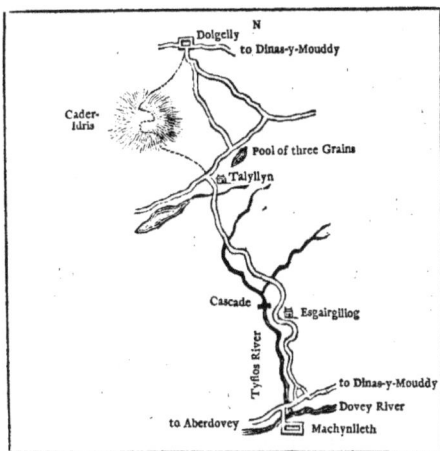

Letter VI

TO THE SAME

DEAR SIR,   *Dolgelly, Aug. 19th.*

Nothing strikes the traveller who passes through Wales more forcibly, than the extreme reasonableness of the bills at houses of public entertainment. Our supper last night was superb; it consisted of a sole, a trout, and a *gwyniad*, (a delicious fish, somewhat like the trout, and peculiar to Alpine countries) with every proper accompaniment; mutton steaks, vegetables, excellent bread and cheese, and three tankards of London porter, "With toast embrown'd, "And fragrant nutmeg fraught, divine repast!" Our beds were comfortable, and the breakfast this morning was fit for a monarch. You will scarcely credit me, when I assure you, the charge for this sumptuous fare and admirable accommodation, amounted only to five shillings and two-pence; which sum was divided into the following items:—

	s.	d.
Supper	2	0
Porter	1	6
Breakfast	1	8
	5	2

This appears the more extraordinary, as the prices of provisions between Wales and England do not differ in any thing like the same proportion with the charges at the inns in the respective countries. We have hitherto found good butcher's meat not to be gotten under sixpence per pound; bread full as dear as in the south, and butter little less expensive. These indeed are unnatural prices in Wales, one unfortunate consequence of the war we are engaged in, which has, in the Principality, raised the article of butcher's meat above one hundred per cent. and added, in an unprecedented manner to the expence of every article of life.[1]

---

1   We found this to be the case entirely through Wales. Till

In our way through the town we looked into its church, the door of which stood open, an ill built, misshapen edifice. At the western end of it was a large gallery where thirty or forty boys, the lads of the town and neighbourhood, were instructed in writing and reading both Welsh and English, during the summer months. We found this practice had been observed here for some years, a circumstance that accounted for our own vernacular tongue being more generally spoken at Machynlleth, than in many other towns at a less distance from England. We passed the Dovy, which flows to the north of Machynlleth and divides it from Merionethshire, over an old stone bridge, from which we were gratified by a sight entirely new to us, the management of *coracles*, and the mode of fishing from them. These little water conveyances are, you know, of high antiquity, receiving their name from the *coria*, or skins, with which they were originally covered. They have now indeed dropt their right to this appellation; a coarse, pitched canvas being substituted as a coating in the room of leather. Intended to carry only one person each, they are not more than five feet long, and four broad, rounded at the corners, and constructed of wicker work; and are consequently sufficiently light to be conveyed on the back of the fisherman to

---

within these six years, mutton was to be bought at 2d. and 24d. per pound, and other meat in proportion; now 5d. and 6d. are commonly given for good joints from Usk to Conway.

his home when the labour of the day is concluded. Simple as this construction is, we find the ancient Britons encountered the waves of the ocean
in them, voyaging in their *wicker baskets covered with leather* to the island Mictis;[2] a perilous
undertaking, whether the name be applicable to
the Isle of Wight, or to one of the Cassiterides.
The man who manages the *coracle* is seated exactly in the centre of it, and directs its motion by
the action of a small paddle, with which it is truly
astonishing how compleatly he commands this
apparently aukward vessel. Two *coracles* usually
go together in order to assist each other in fishing; an operation of singular address and activ-
ity, the right hand being employed all the time
in paddling, the left hand in conducting the net,
and the *teeth* in holding the line attached to it.

We now entered a deep vale, whose beauties
are so multiplied and various, that I really feel
myself unable to describe them with any degree
of justice. The first object that led us from the
road was a roaring cataract, on our left hand,
formed by the torrent of the Dyflàs, which flings
itself with foaming precipitation down this valley. Another more important cascade, on the
same stream, occurred before we had proceeded two miles further. Here the river, struggling
through its craggy bed, falls suddenly from a
ledge about fifteen feet in height, and dashes

---

2   *Ad eam (insulam) Britannos* vitilibus navigijs corio circum-
sutis *navigare.*Plin. *Hist.* I. 4, c. 16.

through a deep and perpendicular rocky chasm, the sides of which are, scooped into semicircular excavations by the ceaseless action of the water. The pure transparency of this delicious stream is such, that the smallest pebble may be clearly seen at the depth of fifteen feet, and we more than once distinguished the rapid course of the trout through it, when we were thirty or forty yards above its level. From hence for three miles the road winds through a country exquisitely beautiful. On the left of the Dyflâs is seen broken into a thousand cascades, now foaming through its stony channel, and now leading its more tranquil waters by verdant meads and flowery banks. A steep hill, luxuriantly covered with timber trees, shoots up to a towering height beyond it, and is opposed by elevations equally stupendous on the right hand, from whose precipitous sides craggy rocks, of enormous magnitude and fantastic form, beetle over the road in a most tremendous manner. This scene was a proper prelude to the view that opened to us at the seventh mile stone from Machynlleth, when Cader-Idris, the majestic father of the Merionethshire mountains, appeared in all his grandeur, literally lifting his black precipices above the clouds. Animated with an impatient desire to explore the wonders of this mountain, we took an hasty view of Tallyllyn pool, a beautiful lake at the southern foot of Cader-Idris, and passed onto a public-house at Minsfordd-Tallyllyn, where we had been directed to procure a guide. The master of it, Edward Jones, a Welshman, whose natural ingenuity had been sharpened into cunning by a long residence in England, after some little instances of imposition, introduced to us a person as our companion and conductor over the mountain. Having therefore provided our selves with some necessary articles of refreshment, we set out, attended by our new acquaintance, Mr. David Pughe, a thick-set little Cambrian between fifty and sixty. We soon found he was a character. His pompous manner and affected dignity were truly diverting, and the triumph with which he dwelt on the antiquity of his family afforded a whimsical example of that harmless pride which the Welsh, with all their excellencies, possess in a higher degree than any of their neighbours. The founder of his stock was, he assured us, an hero who flourished some ages before the Christian epoch; and he affirmed, it appeared by an elaborate genealogy which was made out about three years since, that his race had flowed in an uninterrupted stream for no less than three thousand years!

Leaving the usual road of ascent, we visited a torrent that rushed down the southern side of the mountain, and formed in its course a series of very pleasing cascades. We followed its acclivities, and after an hour's hard labour, reached the vale in which it had its origin, a deep recess called Doly-dd-Cây. Here the heights of Cader-Idris began to shut us in, and seclude us from the sight of every thing but its own lofty precipices. Our walk had not as yet afforded us the sight of the indigenous animal of the country, the goat; we saw them, however, now in perfection, skipping amongst the crags of Cader-Idris, in their original ferine state. Not that they are unclaimed property, since they all belong to some one or other of the neighbouring farmers; but as the proprietor does not use them for domestic purposes, and leaves them to wander for months unmolested, they may be said to preserve the character of their natural wildness. Such is the extent of the mountain, that they are caught with the utmost difficulty, when winter renders it proper to take them home; and the only mode of effecting this, is by pursuing them with cur dogs, which, after a considerable time, literally tire them down. Here too we were desired to observe the rocky coverts where the foxes (numerous amongst these cliffs) took refuge from their bloodthirsty pursuers; and shuddered, whilst Pughe, who was himself "a mighty hunter," gave us an account of those desperate chaces which dogs and men follow, through regions that no lowlander can behold without terror. The sport, however, to those who enjoy it divested of fear, must be most glorious and animating. The rocks and precipices re-echo the united sounds of huntsmen, dogs, and horns, and a chorus is formed singular, striking, and indescribable.

Another half hour brought us into a second valley called Cwm-y-cày, a deep hollow in the heart of the mountain, shut in to the north, west, and south, by huge rocks of porphyry, and black perpendicular precipices of five and six hundred feet in height. The centre of this coomb is filled by a clear and extensive lake, of unfathomable depth, which, together with other surrounding circumstances, give the whole hollow the appearance of an ancient volcanic crater. This piece of water is called Lyn-cây, and according to the account of our companion, covers fifty acres, and is filled with trout of large size and exquisite flavour.

Skirting the southern margin of this pool with some difficulty, we picked up, amongst the fragments of rocks, several specimens of fine calcareous spar, and added to our plants the *Sedum rupestre*, and *Narthecium ossifragum*; and at length approached a dark, beetling rock, of shaggy aspect and tremendous height, which stands entirely detached from the neighbouring cliff. Its real name is Craig-cây, but our guide, with a pardonable vanity, had christened it after himself, and assured us it was called Pughe's pinnacle. Here we were delighted with the magical effects of a fine echo; a howl, or indeed any other sound delivered loudly and deliberately, is reflected from one surface of the rock to another in several repercussions, at one time very clearly and distinctly heard; then fading away to a distant whisper; and again returning upon the ear as if emitted from a neighbouring crag. Arriving at the extremity of the pool, we began to ascend the western summit of Cader-Idris, a task not only of labour, but of some peril also, it being a different route from that which travellers usually pursue; six hundred feet of steep rock, covered, indeed, with short grass, but so slippery as to render the footing very insecure. As we approached the top, the ascent became more abrupt, whilst the scene below us, of craggy rocks, perpendicular precipices, and an unfathomable lake, did not operate to lessen the alarm that a person, unaccustomed to so dangerous a situation, naturally feels. Our companion the mountaineer skipped on, the mean while, with the agility of a goat, and whilst C—— and I were dumb with terror, descanted on the beauties of Cader Idris, the excellence of its mutton, and the delicacy of its trout, as coolly as if he had been in the public-house where we originally found him. At length, after excessive labour, and repeated efforts, we gained the top of this noble mountain, and were at once amply recompensed for all the fatigue and alarm of the ascent. The afternoon was gloriously fine, and the atmosphere perfectly clear, so that the vast unbounded prospect lay beneath us, unobscured by cloud, vapour, or any other interruption to the astonished and delighted eye; which threw its glance over a varied scene, including a circumference of at least five hundred miles. To the north-west is seen Ireland, like a distant mist upon the ocean; and a little to the right, Snowdon and the other mountains of Caernarvonshire. Further on, in the same direction, the Isle of Man, the neighbourhood of Chester, Wrexham, and Salop; the sharp head of the Wrekin, and the undulating summit of the Clee hills. To the south we have the country round Clifton, Pembrokeshire, St. David's, and Swansea; and to the westward, a vast prospect of the British Channel unfolds itself, which is bounded only by the horizon. Exclusive of these distant objects, the nearer views are wonderfully striking. Numberless mountains, of different forms, appearances, and elevation, rise in all directions around us; which, with the various harbours, lakes and rivers, towns, villages, and seats, scattered over the extensive prospect, combine to form a scene inexpressibly august, diversified, and impressive. Having refreshed ourselves with the contents of a knapsack carried by our companion, we proceeded, in an eastern direction, to the Pen-yr-Cader, the highest peak of the mountain, passing on our left the saddle of the giant Idris, (from whom the mountain receives its name) an immense cwm, its bottom filled with a beautiful lake called Llyn Cair, and its sides formed by perpendicular cliffs at least 1000 feet in height. Here we found the Alpine grasses, the *Aira Caspitosa*, and the *Poa Alpina*; beautiful masses of spar, specimens of pyritæ, and a stone much resembling that volcanic substance called pumice-stone. We were now upon the apex of the second mountain in

Wales, in point of height, and 2850 feet above the green, near the neighbouring town of Dolgelly. The air, notwithstanding the rays. of an unclouded sun beamed upon us, was piercingly cold; and as our preceding fatigue had produced a profuse perspiration, we quickly found ourselves chilly and uncomfortable. Having therefore extended our walk half a mile beyond the Pen, and taken a view of two other lakes, Lyn-Mullyn, the Lake of Three Grains, and Lyn-Gawar, or Goat's-pool, we turned about in order to descend the northern side of the mountain. From the rude heap of adventitious stones which form what is called the bed of the giant, for several hundred yards, the mountain wears a singular appearance. Its surface is covered with a stream of rocky fragments of different magnitude, and lying in all directions, their shape for the most part columnar and quadrangular, and many being from three to seven feet in length. All of them bear the marks of attrition, and probably were thrown into their present rude, disjoined situation, by that great convulsion of nature, when "the fountains of the great deep were broken up, and the windows of heaven were opened." Having waded through this flood of stones, and reached the track that leads to Dolgelly, we parted with our good-humoured, whimsical conductor, and winded slowly down the northern side of Cader-Idris, after spending six hours amidst its stupendous scenery. We reached the Golden Lion at eight o'clock, and are preparing to refresh ourselves after the severest fatigue we have yet experienced.

Your's, &c.

R. W.

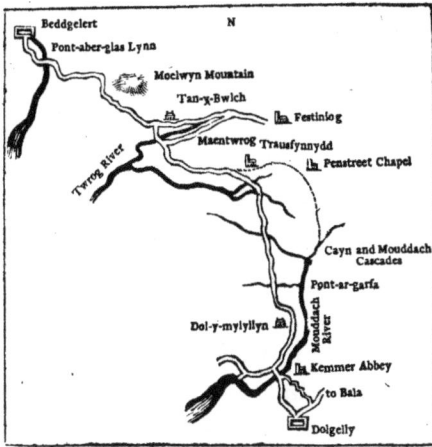

Letter VII

TO THE SAME

DEAR SIR, *Beddgelert, Aug. 19th.*

e rose earlier than usual this morning, after a most comfortless night; during which we had been tormented by fleas, and nearly suffocated by the closeness of a room nine feet by five and a half, into which were crammed two beds, a table, and a chair. Fatigue is, indeed, a powerful opiate, and we dropt asleep notwithstanding all the inconveniences of our situation. Nature, however, took only as much repose as was absolutely necessary for her restoration, and we were awake and up with the first glimpse of day. We had enquired over-night, whether the service of the church were performed at Dolgelly in Welsh or English, and finding it to be in an unknown tongue, we determined to reach Maentwrog (about twenty miles distant) as early as possible, that we might attend the chapel there in the afternoon; where, we were told, it was likely the English Liturgy would be read. Having paid our bill, therefore, we left Dolgelly at six o'clock. The situation of this place is very agreeable, watered by the river Onion,[1] and standing in the midst of fertile meadows. It receives some importance also from being a market for Welsh flannels, which are manufactured in the neighbouring villages, and brought here to be disposed of at the fairs of Dolgelly, to the dealers who resort hither for the purchase of them. The famous Owen Glendower conferred no small dignity on this place, by assembling his parliament here in the year 1404, when he formed an alliance with Charles king of France. The prosperous state of his affairs at that time is sufficiently obvious, from the language of the deed appointing John Hanmer and Griffith Yonge to be his ministers in the business, which runs in this right royal style:—*Owinus Deigratid princeps Wallia*; and concludes, D*atum apud Doleguelli* 10 *die mensis Maii* MCCCC *quarto et principatus nostri quarto:*[2]

---

1   River Wnion. —Ed,

2   Pennant, *North-Wales.*

About a mile from Dolgelly we turned into a narrow lane to the right, in order to take a passing view of the ruined Abbey of Kemmer,[3] a Cistertian monastery dedicated to St. Mary, and founded by an unknown patron about the year 1200. At the Dissolution it was valued only at 51l. 13s. but it seems probable that its property must have decreased considerably (a circumstance which the ecclesiastics seldom allowed to take place) prior to that event, as in the year 1231, during the wars between Henry III. and the prince of Wales, the Abbot of Kemmer was content to give the English 300 marks (a very large sum at that period) in order to save this monastery from conflagration.[4] We were much disappointed when we reached the object of our search; the ruin is a trifling one, and has nothing in it either beautiful, solemn or picturesque. The rain now came on very heavily, and, after passing the bridge that crosses the Mouddach, we were glad to take shelter in Llaneltyd turnpike-house, whither we were kindly invited by its tenant, the man who kept the toll. Not having yet breakfasted, we enquired for an inn where we might be furnished with this necessary meal, and were answered by our host, we should be accommodated at his cottage, and that his daughter would be happy in providing it for us immediately. He accordingly called her, and the young Cambrian made her appearance.

---

3   Cymer Abbey. —Ed.

4   Tanner, *Not. Mon.* 715.

C—— and I agreed we had scarcely ever seen a girl more lovely or interesting. She was tall, and elegantly shaped; her complexion fair, her large blue eyes beaming kindness and benignity; her flaxen hair flowing in negligent ringlets over her shoulders; her voice musically sweet, and her manners wonderfully soft, and greatly superior to the sphere in which she moved. Prepared by so fair a hand, we ate our breakfast with additional relish; and, whilst we were dispatching some of the best home-made cakes and butter I had ever tasted, our honest host entertained us with his history. His name is Henry Roberts, and his native country North-Wales. Early in life he had gone into the army, and, after carrying the musket for many years, retired from the service with some severe wounds, the loss of his right arm, and a Chelsea out-pension. Of late years he had combined several different employments together, and by those means contrived to provide a comfortable subsistence for his wife, his daughter, and himself. By keeping the turnpike he lived rent free, and received a little annual stipend; during the summer he frequently attended travellers to the falls of the Mouddach, and the top of Cader-Idris; and his income was further increased by retailing to the villagers tea, sugar, thread, and the thousand other little articles which constitute the stock of a chandler's shop. We had finished our breakfast before he had concluded his history, for it was told with all the garrulity of seventy, and all the circumstantiality of an old soldier. However, as my companion and myself are not of the number of those who disdain to hear "the simple annals of the poor," we neither hastened nor interrupted the detail, but listened with all proper attention till he had concluded his adventures. When he was fairly come to a close, we asked him if he would accompany us to the neighbouring cataracts; this he immediately consented to do; we therefore took leave of our fair attendant, and quitted Llaneltyd turnpike about half past seven o'clock.

The first cataract to which our guide conducted us was over Dôl-y-Myllyn, situate a little beyond the fifth mile-stone from Dolgelly, near the house of William Madox, esq. Passing through a white gate to the left hand of the road, we approached the fall by a path which climbs a pretty steep acclivity, clothed with trees of various kinds, and sprinkled with numerous uncommon and curious plants. This ascent continues the better part of half a mile, when the fall opens itself to the view. We first observed it from above. Here the water appears to throw itself down a perpendicular descent of full forty feet, in two principal sheets, and thro' some lateral gullies, into an hideous bed of black, disjoined rocks, through which it struggles for a few yards, and is then lost to the spectator in the surrounding woods. To obtain a view of its further progress we struck into a steep and intricate path, which led us to the foot of the cascade, where the scene became much more grand, beautiful, and extensive, than before. An additional fall of twenty-five feet now appears immediately in front; the first cataract, and the ragged channel into which it discharges itself, are seen to the left hand; and to the right, perpendicular rocks crowned with noble trees, which throw their broad arms over the glittering waters, and relieve with sober shade their dazzling splendour. Retracing our path through the coppice, we returned into the road, and proceeding along it, were directed to remark a lofty mountain, which rose immediately on the left hand. It is called the Prince of Wales's mountain, and was formerly the subject of much speculation in the mining way. The veins, however, proved not sufficiently valuable to repay the expences of working them, and were consequently neglected. We in part ascended it, and collected several good mineralogical specimens; such as lumps of lead and copper ore, pieces of spar, micacious stones, and so forth. A curious species of the toad stone also, which abounds in the neighbourhood of this mountain, and is found in vast masses at the bottom of it, attracted our attention; it is of a dull greenish colour and cellular, the chambers filled with a hard substance in appearance exactly like good charcoal. Seven miles from Dolgelly our guide conducted us over a bridge, to the right of the road, called Pont-ar-Garfa, from the river of that name which flows under it. From hence we proceeded nearly two miles on a gradual ascent over a slate mountain, the dullness of which was soon contrasted by a magnificent and sublime prospect. The summit of the hill Tylyn-Gwladys, which we had been ascending, is opposed to the lofty mountain Cwm-Ysom, and the profound valley of Mouddach at its feet. Through this immense hollow the two torrents Cayne and Mouddach pour their irresistible streams; and, though the deep woods which compleatly clothe the declivities on either side, preclude a view of their troubled waters; yet the roar of their cataracts swells upon the gale, and reaches the ear in one continued peal of distant thunder. The solemn sentiments which this circumstance naturally inspires, were exalted and enlivened, as we descended, by the surrounding scenery; the umbrageous and gloomy appearance of the glen, the precipitous declivity of the hills, and the sharp rocky crags which shoot through the verdant clothing of their sides. An infinite variety of shrubs and trees planted by the hand of nature, but disposed with the justest taste and happiest effect, compleat the beauty of this fairy region; the trembling foliage of the aspen; the vivid berries of the mountain ash; and the melancholy shade of the pendent birch.

Our first object was the Pistil-y-Cayne, or fall of the Cayne; in order to approach which, we passed over a rude Alpine bridge, formed of the trunk of an oak, thrown from rock to rock, and hanging frightfully over a black torrent that roared many feet beneath it. We descended with some difficulty to the bottom of the fall. Here the effect is very august. A sheet of water is seen pouring down a rugged declivity, nearly perpendicular, of two hundred feet; the view of it compleat and full, uninterrupted by the adjoining woods, which, though they thickly mantle its sides, do not break by the intervention of their branches the continuity of the fall. After tumbling from this stupendous height, the agitated waters are received amongst rocks of a light dun colour, which their perpetual action has excavated into hollows of alarming profundity and various shapes, and through these they force their course, in order to unite themselves with the Mouddach, a few hundred yards from the spot on which we stood. Whilst we were contemplating this grand example of nature's magnificence, the sun, who had hitherto veiled his head in clouds, shone suddenly and full upon the descending sheet of water, and produced an appearance that conveyed no bad idea of an immense shower of diamonds falling from an eminence. After some time spent on this scene, we were led to the Pistily-Mouddach, or fall of the Mouddach, which it was necessary for us to view from beneath, as it is impracticable to attain its summit. This cataract is of a character compleatly different from any we have before visited. Indeed, we may extend this remark to all the particulars of Welsh scenery; each spot having, as it were, a character peculiar to itself, a circumstance which produces inexhaustible variety, and constant sources of fresh entertainment to the admirer of nature. The Pistil-y-Mouddach consists of three falls, submitted at one view to the eye. The first is a sheet of water about twenty feet wide, and nearly as many in height, which tumbles into a deep pool of thirty feet in diameter. From hence it glides over a second ledge, producing a fall of about thirty feet, into another bason of larger dimensions. Here contracting itself, it is discharged by a third fall of twenty feet into the largest and deepest pool, over the brim of which it soon boils into a rude congeries of rocky crags, and foams forward to its point of junction with the Cayne, affording an example of the accuracy with which the poet of nature has painted this, amongst her other varied scenes:

> Smooth to the shelving brink a copious flood
> Rolls fair and placid, where, collected all,
> In one impetuous torrent down the steep
> It thund'ring shoots, and shakes the country round.
> At first an azure sheet, it rushes broad;
> Then whitening by degrees as prone it falls,
> And from the loud-resounding rocks below
> Dash'd in a cloud of foam, it sends aloft
> A hoary mist, and forms a ceaseless shower.
> Nor can the tortur'd wave here find repose,
> But raging still amid the shaggy rocks,
> Now flashes o'er the scatter'd fragments, now
> A slant the hollow'd channel rapid darts,
> And falling fast from gradual slope to slope,

With wild infracted course and lessen'd roar,
It gains a safer bed, and steals at last
Along the mazes of the quiet vale
                    THOMSON'S *Summer.*

On either side of this fall the mountains rise abruptly to the height of 7 or 800 feet, darkened by the shade of deep woods, but occasionally shewing the white face of the rock. This is more especially the case with one steep, which has occasioned it to be called Gwin-Mynnydd or the white mountain. Our guide having conducted us through the intricacies of the wood, placed us in an open country, and given us directions for our progress, took his leave and returned to Llaneltyd. The day, in the mean time, was again become dark, wet, and uncomfortable, and heightened the desolation and gloom of a barren, mountainous country, in which not a single interesting object occurred, either natural or artificial, to relieve or enliven the dolorous monotony of the scene. After having consumed an hour in this way, we saw before us a solitary building, which appeared to be a long, low cottage. On our approach towards it, we were suddenly surprised by the notes of harmony;

A solemn-breathing sound
Rose like a steam of rich distill'd perfumes,
And stole upon the air; that even Silence
Was took 'ere she was 'ware, and wish'd she might
Deny her nature, and be never more,
Still to be so displac'd.

We listened attentively, and were delighted with the melody, which was as striking as unexpected. It seemed to be a religious hymn, sung by a great number of voices, for the most part sweet and harmonious. Solemn and simple, it was not, like our church-music, interrupted by pauses at the conclusion of each line and stanza, but continued, and without a break; varied only by fine swells and dying falls, and the regular observation of the piano and the forte. We drew near to the building, and perceiving we occasioned no disturbance, joined ourselves to the congregation. The scene was a striking and a pleasing one. A number of people, who must have come from far, neat in their dress, devout in their manner, were collected together in a hovel upon a barren mountain, to sing the psalm of thanks giving, to breathe the prayer of simplicity, and to worship their Maker in spirit and in truth; the pastor, an elderly man of respectable appearance, unaffected in his manner, fervent in his petitions, solemn, impressive, and energetic in his exhortations! Such was the scene which this cottage exhibited. And neither C—— nor myself were insensible to its influence. Their divine harmony penetrated our souls; and though unacquainted with the language in which their thanks givings were conveyed, we lifted up our thoughts to heaven with a devotion of mind which we trust the Being who knows all hearts, and who marks each secret aspiration of them for his favour, will accept, in lieu of our customary mode of social worship on this day, which we were prevented from joining in by the circumstances of our situation. When the service was concluded, we made some enquiries relative to the place, the preacher, and the sect to which he belonged. Our curiosity was satisfied by the female inhabitant of a little cottage attached to one end of the chapel, who spoke extremely good English, and exhibited a perfect pattern of neatness and simplicity. From her we understood the hamlet was called Penstreet appropriated to a congregation of Presbyterians, who assembled here every Sunday, and were instructed by the Rev. Mr. Wm. Jones, a man of great respectability and exemplary character.

Nothing, perhaps, can afford a stronger or more agreeable instance of that religious spirit which prevails amongst the lower orders of Welsh, than the circumstance I have just related to you;—a congregation collecting together at a chapel situated in a wild, mountainous country, and considerably distant from the nearest habitation, and that too in defiance of the rain and the wind, which had fallen and blown through all the morning with little intermission. To this religious spirit, indeed, may be attributed that humanity, courtesy, and decency, which the Welsh possess in so superior a degree to the English candille; for it is a truth which candour and observation will readily allow, that the only foundation for good morals and decent conduct, at least amongst the lower orders, is a principle of religion, a knowledge of the duties it teaches, and a sense of their obligation to perform them, as rational and accountable beings.

The waning day was very unfavourable for the delicious prospect which opened upon us about a mile from Tan-y-Bwlch. Here the beautiful vale of Festiniog spread itself to the eye, comprehending every object that can enrich or diversify a landscape. Noble mountains rising on every side, some thickly mantled with wood, others lifting their bare, rocky heads into the clouds. A meandring river rolling through extensive meads, which its fertilizing waters clothe with constant verdure. The picturesque chapel and neat cottages of Maentwrog, occupying the centre of the vale; and the elegant seat of Mr. Oakley, called Tan-y Bwlch hall, with its noble woods decorating the declivity of a mountain on the northern side. Here, for the first time since we have been in North-Wales, we were gratified in seeing the spirit of agricultural improvement exerted to some extent, and with considerably good effect. The vale of Festiniog consists in general of a soil rather mossy and spungy, the consequence of having formerly been always overflowed at spring tides. Aware of the injury which these inundations occasioned to the land, Mr. Oakley determined to prevent them by embankments. Having effected this, he next turned his attention to draining the ground thus secured, which he did so effectually as to render its produce just triple to what it hitherto had been. His large drains and neat embankments rather adorn than injure the picture; as the former are like small canals, and the latter have the appearance of raised terrace walks, surmounted with a neat white rail.

We were now extremely wet, and very well inclined to seat ourselves by a comfortable fireside; you will therefore imagine our disappointment, when the host of Tan-y-Bwlch inn told us we could neither be provided with a dinner, nor accommodated with beds at his house. There is a mode, you know, of imparting unpleasant intelligence, which, if it do not lessen the evil told, leaves us at least in good-humour with the person who tells it. The landlord of Tan-y-Bwlch inn, however, was either unacquainted with this art of softening the disagreeable, or at least did not chuse to exercise it; for he communicated his information in a manner so ungracious, as to fix an indelible impression on our minds of his being a very surly fellow. It was now six o'clock in the evening, and we had eight miles to walk over the wildest and most desolate road in all Wales. We therefore quickened our pace, and wound up the mountains that overlook the vale of Festiniog to the north. Nothing can exceed the desolation and rudeness of the scene for the first five or six miles. Bare rocks, and fragments of mountains, divested of tree or shrub, are thrown about in the wildest confusion. No vestige of a dwelling, no trace of human society occurs. It wears the appearance of a country shaken and overturned by the powerful operation of internal convulsions, and from which all animated nature has fled dispersed and alarmed. A thick mist, which occasionally involved us, added to the effect of the scene, and allowed the fancy to indulge in all the reveries of imaginary horror. The only relief we had to this lengthened gloom, was a prospect which opened to the left, on our gaining an elevation at the fourth mile-stone; the fog at the same time clearing away, and allowing us to enjoy it. Here we caught the Traeth Bach, (the mouth of the river Dwy'ryd that waters Festiniog) Cardigan Bay, and the ocean beyond it; the town of Barmouth; the ruins of Harlech Castle; the lofty summit of the solitary Penmorfa; and the pointed heads of other maritime mountains. This variation of scene, however; was but of short duration; the road again descended, and led us once more into the same heap of natural ruins as before. At length we were gratified with the sight of Pont-aber-glas-Lyn (the bridge of the harbour of the blue lake) which we had been anxiously expecting to reach for some time. It is a single arch, built over a rapid mountain torrent that divides the two counties of Merioneth and Caernarvon. The features of this romantic spot are well pourtrayed by Mr. Wyndham, [*Tour*, p. 125.] of whose description I shall avail myself, as it is probable my own pencil would not afford you so true a likeness:

"Here we paused," says he,

while the grandeur of the scene before us impressed a silent admiration on our senses. We, at length, moved slowly onwards, contemplating the wonderful chasm. An impending craggy cliff, at least 800 feet high, projects, from every part of its broken front, stupendous rocks of the most capricious forms, and shadows a broad translucid torrent, which rages like a cataract amid the huge ruins fallen from the mountain.

On the opposite declivity, the disjointed fragments, crushing their mouldering props, seem scarcely prevented from overwhelming the narrow ridge, which forms the road on the brink of the flood.

The excentric and romantic imagination of Salvator Rosa was never fired with a more tremendous idea, nor has his pencil ever produced a bolder precipice.

The bridge of Aberglaslyn connects two perpendicular precipices with a semicircular arch of stone, the diameter of which is thirty feet, and the crown of the arch is forty feet above the water level. Just above it the whole river falls down a craggy break, of the height of about twelve feet. This is called the Salmon Leap, and our attention was many times diverted from the majestic scenery around us, by the dexterity of the salmons leaping over it. The fishery here is very ancient, and, in the history of the Gwider family, is called the King's Weare; it is mentioned by that title in some old records of the time of Henry IV.

C—— and I waited on the bridge for a considerable time, in order to see the fish perform the feat of agility above described; only two, however, attempted it, and neither of them with success. Indeed, we had heard from a gentleman whom we met at the Devil's-Bridge, that the object of this leap is seldom effected. He had continued some hours on the bridge, during which time nearly seven-score fish endeavoured to throw themselves up the fall, but not one in twenty appeared to succeed.

We looked into the level of the copper-mine penetrating the left hand mountain, which belongs to Sir W. W. Wynne, and is said to produce purer ore than the Paris mine; and then pursued our walk along a road that runs under an immense precipice, nearly perpendicular, parallel with the torrent Colwyn. This conducted us to Beddgelert, a village at the foot of Snowdon, where civil treatment, good accommodation, and comfortable cheer, have made amends for all the inconvenience and disappointment of the past day.

Your's, &c.

R. W.

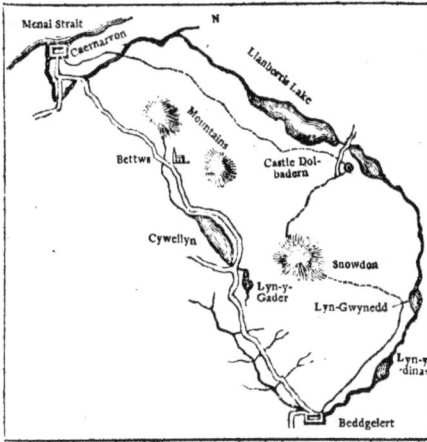

Letter VIII

TO THE SAME

DEAR SIR,   *Caernarvon, Aug. 21th.*

ne great object of our expedition was, you know, to traverse Snowdon and its dependencies; to visit the summit of the highest mountain in the three kingdoms. We were therefore much disappointed on being informed this morning by the guide, who lives at the village inn during the summer in the capacity of waiter, that the day was unfavourable for our attempt, the head of the mountain being involved in impenetrable mist. It was vain to lament what could not be remedied; we therefore determined to make the best of a misfortune, and spend the day in visiting some other magnificent scenery, which would have been incompatible with our expedition to the top of Snowdon. We accordingly agreed with the guide, William Lloyd, an intelligent man, to accompany us a few miles, and quitted our quarters about nine o'clock. Our road conducted us along the bank of the little river *Wu* (the ancient Welsh name for water) which flowed on our right hand, to the beautiful pool of Llyn-y-dinas,[1] stretching a mile and half in length; the dark-brown mountains Arran[2] [stone] and Lliweddy,[3] rising to a stupendous height on the left. Here our guide directed us to turn round, and observe an huge perpendicular rocky mountain, finely shaded with wood, which we had left behind. He told us it was called Dinâs-Emris, and received its name from the famous old British magician Merlin, or Merddin Emries, who, seated on its cloud-capt head, had formerly prophesied to the unfortunate Vortigern all the evils which afterwards befel him self, his kingdom, and his degenerate subjects.[4] The summit of Snowdon, towering above us to the north, had hitherto been involved in a fleecy cloud, which

---

1   Llyn Dinas. —Ed.

2   Y Aran. —Ed.

3   Y Lliwedd. —Ed.

4   Mr. Pennant in his *Snowdonia*, p. 175, has given the legend of Dinâs Emris at length.

hung around it in the manner of a curtain, undulating with the wind. This now appeared to be drawn up higher than it had yet been; and to rest like a crown on the very point of the mountain. Our guide having attentively regarded it for some time, gave it as his opinion that we should have an opportunity of prosecuting our original plan, the misty mantle being likely to melt away altogether before the sun, which was now approaching towards his meridian. He observed, however, at the same time, that should we determine to visit the top of Snowdon, we should find the ascent from the point where we stood to be much more steep and disagreeable than the regular road would have been from the inn at which we had slept; that, notwithstanding, it was a practicable way, and had been trodden by some travellers before us. We instantly resolved on attempting the ascent, and having, by his advice, swallowed a draught of milk at a neighbouring cottage, and replenished our "leathern bottels" with some of the same beverage, we began the toilsome undertaking. The first stage of our journey was up a rugged steep, by the side of a mountain torrent, which, falling from ledge to ledge, stunned us with its unceasing noise. The principal branch of the Arran, little inferior to his mighty neighbour, heaved his unwieldly bulk into the clouds on the right hand, under which a frightful hollow, called Cwm-Llan, spread its hideous profundity, stretching a mile and half in

length, and nearly as much in breadth, a precipice of Snowdon forming one of its black perpendicular sides. While we contemplated this
scene with marks of astonishment and dread,
the guide related an anecdote to us, which was
no bad satire upon the impressions of alarm that
C—— and myself felt in this aërial situation.
He told us, the farm we had passed in the bottom was called Llan farm, and had been occupied, till within these few years, by Mr. William
Griffiths, the father of the present tenant. That
the old man attended constantly the market of
Caernarvon, and in order to avoid a route rather circuitous by the turnpike-road, he constantly
crossed the mountain by the track which we had
pursued, mounted on a little poney of the country, that crawled up with him through the crags,
and bogs, and steeps of this side, and descended on the other by a road equally rude, abrupt,
and rocky. That day or night, light or darkness
made no alteration in his system, which he pursued for many years without experiencing injury
or accident. It may be properly observed, however, that in this perilous expedition he was more
indebted to his horse than to himself for safety;
and indeed, nothing but actual observation can
give a just idea of that sure-footedness and caution which the little Welsh ponies possess; that
faculty of mounting acclivities, and descending
steeps, through fragments of rock, and other ob-
structions, that appear to render the mountain

paths impassable. After two hours of very severe labour we gained the summit of Snowdon,[5] (a sharp narrow crag of rock, not more than two yards over) and stood 3568 feet above the level of Caernarvon quay. Our toil, however, seemed at first to be but ill repaid; a crown of clouds still covered the top, and we remained involved in a mist that produced the most intense cold. We now produced our bottles of milk, which we found very grateful and refreshing, but regretted at the same time that we had not some stronger cordial. Our guide, indeed, soon reconciled us to the absence of any powerful liquors, by assuring us they were more productive of danger than comfort; as a very small quantity of them in these etherial regions was sufficient to intoxicate. He mentioned his having nearly fallen from one of the precipices himself, in consequence of drinking a glass of brandy; and that during the preceding summer, one of a party of London gentlemen had been so affected by the same quantity, taken on the summit of Snowdon, that he actually got a severe tumble, so much with a

---

5   The ancient name of Snowdon was Eryrri, or Eagle, from its stupendous crags being occasionally visited by that bird. Its highest pen is called Wyddfa, or the conspicuous. The origin of the English appellation is obvious; the sharp air of the mountain occasioning the snow to lie a long time on its summit, frequently till the middle of June. Such was the information of our guide but, on consulting Mr. Pennant, I find he gives the ancient name differently, Creigie'r Eira, the snowy mountains.—*Snowdonia*, 171.

view to comfort the traveller, as to indulge that propensity in themselves for strong liquors, so common amongst the lower orders of people. A bottle of milk and water, however, with a small portion of brandy in it, will be found to be much more refreshing and agreeable, than undiluted spirits, and not likely to be attended with the unpleasant effects that an incautious use of them may produce. In this truly hyperborean climate we waited half an hour, at the instigation of our guide, who assured us the cloud would shortly leave the head of the mountain;

Vix ea fatus erat, quum circumfusa repentè
Scindit se nubes, et in æthera pergat apertum.[6]

The mist gradually sailed away, and left us to contemplate for a few minutes, a wide, unbounded prospect, diversified with mountains, and vallies, cities, lakes, and oceans. It was not, however, dissimilar to the view from Cader Idris, except that the Wicklow rocks, the bold opposing cliffs of Ireland, were more distinctly seen, and the little Isle of Man made a more conspicuous figure. We were not long indulged with this free, uninterrupted gaze; the cloud again came rolling on from the ocean, and once which, though not fatal, produced some painful bruises. I mention this circumstance as a caution to you, should you visit

---

6   Scarcely had she got out, when suddenly she was surrounded The cloud splits itself, and continues open into the ether. —Ed.

these aërial heights. The guides, in general, make a point of recommending a quantity of spirits to be carried up, as an antidote against the effects of a raw and chilly atmosphere, but in reality, not more infolded us in its chilly embrace. The covering soon became thicker and darker than hitherto, and our guide warned us to descend with all expedition, lest we should be involved in a storm amid these exposed unsheltered regions. We accordingly proceeded through the gloom, following the steps of our conductor, who walked immediately before us, as we literally could not see the distance of a dozen feet. The situation was new to us, and brought to our recollection, the noble passage with which a prophecy of Joel magnificently opens: "A day of darkness and of gloominess, a day of clouds and of thick darkness, as the morning spread upon the mountains;" it produced however, an effect that was very sublime. Occasional gusts of wind, which now roared around us, swept away for a moment, the pitchy cloud that involved particular spots of the mountain, and discovered immediately below us, huge rocks, abrupt precipices, and profound hollows, exciting emotions of astonishment and awe in the mind, which the eye, darting down an immense descent of vacuity and horror, conveyed to it under the dreadful image of inevitable destruction. At the conclusion of another hour we congratulated each other on having reached the bottom of this noble mountain, after seeing it in all its beauty, and all its sublimity, and gathering from its sides some fine specimens of calcareous spar, pyritæ, and mountain crystal. Our guide now left us, and we proceeded towards Dolbadern Castle, which, with the lake Llanberris,[7] came within the intended scheme of our day's observations. After walking, or rather stumbling, over masses of rock for two hours, we reached a cottage situated amidst some coarse meadows, the sparing produce of which the labourers were at this late period getting in. Uncertain what direction to pursue to Dolbadern Castle, we enquired of a woman who stood at the cottage gate, but received no other answer, than an intimation that she did not speak English. After all the expressive gesticulations we could think of, and pronouncing the name of the place with every possible variation of accent, we made her comprehend our meaning; and she ordered her daughter, a girl about twelve years old, to direct us to Castél Dolbàthren. Our little guide tripping on before us like a lapwing, and without the incumbrance of shoe or stocking, led us over rocks and bogs for about two miles, when we found ourselves on the margin of the lake Llanberris, and near the old fortress of Dolbadern. This piece of water is divided by a small field, through which, however, there is a communication by means of a narrow stream, into two lakes, the northern one being the larger, and stretching

---

7   Llanberis is the village. The main lake is Llyn Padarn, next to
     which is Llyn Peris. —Ed.

nearly three miles in length; the latter called, after the castle, lake Dolbadern,[8] and measuring little more than one. Upon the summit of a hill rising at the southern extremity of lake Llanberris stand the ruins of Dolbadern Castle, forming a good accompaniment to the rude and desolate scenery that surrounds it. The only remains of the original fortress consist of the foundations of the exterior buildings, and the greater part of the citadel or keep. This is a circular building, thirty feet in diameter, containing four apartments, the dungeon at the bottom, and three others in succession over it, the ascent to which is by spiral staircases. By whom it was erected does not appear, though it certainly belonged to the ancient Welsh princes, and is consequently of high antiquity.[9] Owen Goch, the unsuccessful rebel, and opponent of his brother Llewellyn, being taken prisoner by the prince, languished twenty years within its walls; and in the long contest which Owen Glendower maintained with Henry IV. and his son, Dolbadern Castle was occasionally in the possession of each party, and considered as an important defence to the interior of Snowdon. It is constructed of the schistus of the country, and though of small extent, is well situated, and was originally very strong. On the declivity of the mountain, immediately facing the castle,

---

8   Llyn Peris. —Ed.

9   It was built in either the 1220s or the 1230s by Llywelyn the Great —Ed.

are considerable quarries of a fine purple slate, the property of Lord Penrhyn, which is conveyed from hence by water to the extremity of lake Llanberris, and afterwards by land-carriage to Caernarvon quay, where it is shipt off for various parts. In the same neighbour hood also is a valuable copper-mine, consisting of four or five levels, penetrating the mountain to various depths. The ore, which is extremely rich, but not procured in any considerable quantity, is sent to Caernarvon by a similar conveyance with the slate.

Having gratified our curiosity at this spot, we dismissed our conductress with a reward for her trouble, and turned into a regular road, which led to Caernarvon, and was the first we had seen in the course of the day. Like all the other mountain roads, however, it consisted entirely of large loose stones, and pointed, solid rock, not a little incommodious to pedestrians who had already followed the undulations of this hilly country for twenty miles. Another hour brought us to the river Ryddell,[10] which flows from the northern extremity of Llanberris lake, and pursues a winding course to Caernarvon. We crossed it by means of a stone bridge, rude in appearance, and unworkmanlike in construction, but which (from the following tablet in its centre) should seem to have been considered as a noble specimen of art at least by the rare genius that built it: *Harry Parry*, the *modern Inigo*, erected this bridge An. Dni. 17—. The day

10   Afon Rhythallt. —Ed.

now drew towards a close, and the unclouded sun, sinking gradually to the ocean, produced a magic scene, which nature only exhibits in countries where she prints her boldest characters. A fine fleecy cloud was drawn around the mountains we had left, and curtained in its embrace nearly half their height. On this, the declining orb of day threw its rich, departing radiance, and displayed an illumination that neither pencil nor pen can imitate or describe: the misty covering of the mountains every moment varied its tint: it now assumed the appearance of a fleece of azure; the next minute it brightened into a rich golden colour; shortly afterwards, it took a deeper yellow. As the sun approached the wave, its tinge changed successively to a brilliant red, and solemn purple, and at length, when he sunk from the horizon, it became gradually colourless and dark. The effect was further heightened by the variation which the cloud exhibited in its form. For a short time it would confine itself to the higher regions of the mountains; then sinking considerably, would nearly encircle their base; and again rising and condensing itself, it hung upon their summits like a crown of glory. The picture on the opposite side was equally beautiful and grand. The solemn turrets of Caernarvon Castle, contrasted with the gay scenery of ships and villas in its neighbourhood, formed the foreground; to the left appeared the dark precipices of the Rivals, three mountains of great bulk, and immense height, which were now in the shade; and beyond them, the ocean, glitering with the rays of the departing sun, stretched as far as the vision extended. Nothing could exceed the glory of his setting; as he approached the waves, his radiance became more tolerable, and his form more distinct, exhibiting the appearance of an immense ball of fire. When he reached the ocean, he seemed to rest upon it, as upon a throne, for a moment, and then buried his splendid rotundity in its waters; reminding us of that beautiful apostrophe to the orb of light, and sublime description, in the father of Erse poetry:—

> Hast thou left thy blue course in heaven, golden-haired son of the sky! The west has opened its gates; the bed of thy repose is there. The waves come to be hold thy beauty. They lift their trembling heads. They see thee lovely in thy sleep; they shrink away with fear. Rest in thy shadowy cave, O sun! Let thy return be with joy.

Indulging those sentiments of wonder and delight which this new and glorious scene had excited in us, we walked slowly on, in silent meditation, to Caernarvon, which we reached at nine o'clock, and reposed ourselves at the King's-Head inn.

Your's, &c.

R. W.

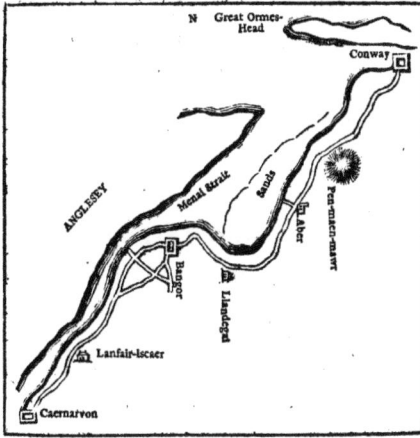

Letter IX

TO THE SAME

DEAR SIR,   *Conway, Aug. 22d.*

o man can justly estimate the value of a good bed, unless he have experienced the discomfort of a very bad one. C—— and I were alive to this enjoyment last night, for during the preceding 100 miles, our nocturnal accommodation has been far from tolerable. This circumstance, indeed, is the only drawback on the pleasure of a Welsh tour; if the country could but boast good beds, Wales would be a paradise.

Having much to do, we rose early, and dispatching an excellent breakfast, sallied into the town, which we had not been able to survey on the preceding evening.

Caernarvon rose on the ruins of the ancient Roman Segontium, but dates the origin of its splendour from the time of Edward I. The English monarch, having conquered the North Wallians, enlarged the town of Caernarvon, and strengthened it with a superb and extensive castle, in order to awe into subjection a fierce people, ardently attached to liberty, who wore the yoke of a foreign master with disgust and impatience. The disagreeable obligation of forging chains for themselves, was imposed on the people of Wales; the peasantry being employed in building the castle, and the chieftains required to defray the expences of it. In the course of one year it was begun and finished, and Elinor, the faithful partner of Edward, gave a young prince to the ancient Britons in one of its apartments, on the 25th of April in the year succeeding its completion.

The castle of Caernarvon is unquestionably a fine specimen of ancient military architecture, but it does not produce those lively emotions in the mind, which edifices of this nature are apt to excite, from the circumstance of its being kept in nice repair, and inhabited. The idea of its high antiquity and ancient splendour is interrupted and destroyed by the patchwork of modern reparation, and the littlenesses of a cottager's domestic œconomy seen within its walls. Exclusive of this, it wants the fine circumstance of a mantle of ivy to relieve, and soften down the displeasing red tinge which it receives from the stone used in erecting it. Its towers are certainly very beautiful, being polygonal, and surmounted with light and elegant turrets. The great entrance is equally striking, a lofty gateway under a stupendous tower, in the front of which appears a gigantic statue of the Conqueror, grasping in his right hand a dagger. The town is neat and cheerful, and not destitute of good houses. One very large and ancient edifice attracted our attention; it is called the Plas Mawr, or great house, and appears to have been the residence of the Lord of the Manor. Two dates, in conspicuous plates, notify that it was built during the years 1590 and 1591; and, indeed, it affords a good specimen of the aukward style of architecture of that time, which was neither Gothic nor classical, but an heterogeneous mixture of both.

We quitted Caernarvon about nine o'clock, and pursued the turnpike-road to Bangor, the view from which, on either side, is equally striking, though entirely different. On the right we had the grand mountain scenes which I have before described; on the left, the beautiful strait called the Menai, separating Anglesey from Wales, and beyond it the ancient seat of Druidical superstition, smiling now with cultivation, and its shore decorated with elegant villas: Plâs

Newydd, the fine seat of Lord Uxbridge; Baron Hill, the residence of Lord Bulkley; and many others; the ocean, bounded only by the sky, finishing the scene. It was a morning of Ossian, and gave the varied view in all its beauty. Morning returned in joy. The "mountains shewed their grey heads; the blue face of ocean smiled. The white wave is seen tumbling round the distant rock." This agreeable prospect continued for five miles, when the Menai, making a sudden sweep to the northward, disappeared for a time. The loss, however, was recompensed by some magnificent additions to the picture, such as the craggy head of the enormous Pen-maen-maur, the huge peninsula of the two Ormes; and the steep, circular island of Priestholme, or Puffin's island. The neat little town of Bangor also, and its surrounding romantic scenery, produced a pleasing effect in the bottom to which we descended. An extremely neat inn, the sign of the Three Eagles, tempted us to refresh ourselves with some of the excellent porter which a board over the door notified might be found within. We requested a tankard of it, therefore, and, whilst quaffing its refreshing stream, learnt from Mr. Hutchings, the intelligent master of the house, many particulars relative to the town and neighbourhood. After a rest of half an hour, we strolled into the church-yard, and surveyed the cathedral. It is a small, low building, of no great antiquity, erected by Bishop Skeffington, in the early part of the sixteenth century. The munificence of the present prelate[1] has, at a great expence, put it into compleat repair, and fitted it up in a style of the most commendable neatness and simplicity. He has also established a regulation with respect to the service in the cathedral, that accommodates both the Welsh and English, by having the offices performed during the forenoon in one language, and in the afternoon in the other. The episcopal palace is immediately behind the cathedral, and the deanery at its western end; both humble, unostentatious mansions, and suitable to the scenery around, which is quiet, peaceful, and highly picturesque. The beauty, retirement, and repose of the whole pleased us wonderfully, and C——— observed, that if *he* were B——— p of Bangor the only *translation* he should covet would be from thence to *Heaven!* I could not but agree with him, that were fate to throw me also into such a spot, very few attractions would have sufficient force to elicit me from it; I should quit the "madding croud" without a sigh, and say, in the language of philosophic pensiveness,

> Here let Time's creeping winter shed
> His hoary snow around my head;
> And while I feel by fast degrees,
> My sluggard blood wax chill and freeze,
> Let thought unveil to my fix'd eye

---

1   John Warren (1730 - 1800), Bishop of Bangor from 1783 till his death. —Ed.

The scenes of deep eternity:
Till, life dissolving at the view,
I wake, and find the vision true

Bangor, you know, is the scite of the ancient Roman station *Bovium*; and many evidences of its being so have been discovered at different times, such as coins, *fibulæ*, &c. In the Saxon period it was no less remarkable, as containing the most populous monastery, perhaps, in the world. Under the British princes from the fourth to the seventh century, the monastery of Bangor consisted of between two and three thousand monks, who passed their hours in manual labour, and the offices of devotion. With the true independent spirit of ancient Britons, they strenuously withstood the usurpation of the church of Rome, under its missionary Augustine, and resisted the imposition of all foreign rites. The Saint could not brook this contumelious obstinacy, and threatened the Monks with his vengeance. Nor were his menaces vain. He shortly after instigated Edilfred, the Saxon king of Northumberland, to invade the kingdom of Powis, of which Bangor formed a part. Brocmail Yscitroc, its prince, raised anarmy to repel him, and ordered 1200 of the Bangorian Monks, to ascend a hill, in sight of the armies, and offer up their prayers for his success during the engagement. These, however, were ineffectual, and Edilfred, after routing the British army, and murdering their useless auxiliaries, proceeded to the monastery, razed it to the ground, and massacred all its unresisting inhabitants.[2]

The town of Bangor, though small, is neat and clean, and watered by "Deva's wizard stream,"[3] which flow sunder an elegant bridge of five arches. This river springs from the foot of the mountain Rauranvaur in Merionethshire, and discharges itself into the Irish sea at Chester, after a long and circuitous course. It is famous in British song, and British story; the fruitful father of superstition, the scene of magic, and of omens. Many wonders were attributed to it, on account of its anciently dividing the principality of Wales from England; and tradition asserted that it frequently varied its fords, previous to any change befalling either country. Thus sang Drayton the topographical poet:

> Again Dee's holiness began
> By his contracted front and sterner waves to shew,
> That he had things to speak that profit them to know:
> A brook that was suppos'd much business to have seen,
> Which had an ancient bound 'twixt Wales and England been,
> And noted was by both to be an ominous flood,
> That changing of his fords, the future ill or good
> Of either country told; of either's war or peace;
> The sickness or the health, the dearth or the increase.
> POLYOLBION, Song 2d.

---

2   Bede's *Ecc. Hist.* 1. 11.

3   The River Dee; *Afon Dyfrdwy* in Welsh, and *Deva Fluvius* in Latin. —Ed.

And Spenser has made its source the scene of conference between the magician Merlin and old Timon:

> Under the foote of Rauran mossy hore,
> From whence the river Dee, as silver cleene,
> His tombling billows rolls with gentle rore.
> FAERIE QUEENE, i. ix

We left Bangor with strong impressions in its favour, having never seen a place which united so many beauties in so narrow a circle; the sublime mountains of Caernarvonshire at a short distance from it; the picturesque scenery of its own immediate neighbourhood; and the ocean spreading its broad bosom within two miles of the town. Add to this, also, the important circumstance of its being one of the cheapest towns in the three kingdoms, and few others will appear to be so inviting and desirable for a residence as Bangor.

Pursuing the turnpike-road to Conway for three miles, we turned into the park of Penrhyn Castle, the noble seat of the peer of that title. It is an ancient edifice, but has of late years undergone a thorough reparation, under the direction of the judicious Wyat, who, with his usual taste and science, has preserved in his improvements, the characteristic style of the military Gothic. About a mile to the south of the castle, on an elevation that overlooks the river Ogwen, stands the little church of Llandegai, built probably about the time of Edward III. The structure is Gothic, exactly cruciform, with a tower in the centre, and exhibits the smallest and neatest example of that figure I ever saw. On the south side of the altar is a large and highly-ornamented alabaster tomb, on the flat slab of which recline the figures of an armed knight and his lady, the latter in the dress of the fourteenth century, their feet resting on a lamb.

We soon approached the enormous promontory Pen-maen-maur, and began to wind up its awful side. The road over this rocky mountain, which was formerly extremely rude and dangerous, has for some years since, under the authority of Parliament and the direction of Mr. Silvester, been entirely altered, and divested of a considerable degree of its horror. Still, however, it cannot be travelled without shuddering. Creeping round the side of the mountain, it hangs as it were in the mid-air, with a frowning precipice above, and a steep descent immediately under it. The rocks on the right are nearly perpendicular, sometimes beetling over the road in a terrific manner, at others retiring into deep declivities of 900 or 1000 feet in height; from whose ragged sides project fragments of incalculable magnitude, so capriciously placed, and having such a disjoined appearance, that it is impossible for the traveller to lose the perpetual dread of his being every moment crushed to atoms under a torrent of huge stones. This danger, indeed, can never be entirely removed, as the united exertions of all the workmen in the world could never clear the face of the mountain from these innumerable masses. A lapse of this kind had happened a day or two before our passing the road, which would inevitably have swept us into the ocean, had we been within the sphere of its violence. Several workmen were employed in repairing the breach it had occasioned in the wall that runs along the edge of the precipice at the left hand of the road, and from the devastation it had there made, we saw awful proofs of its magnitude and force.

Some singular accidents which occurred on the road, previous to the judicious alteration of it in 1772, are preserved in the recollection of the neighbourhood. The following is the most extraordinary one, which I give you on the authority of a most entertaining traveller, an excellent naturalist, and amiable man, who mentions it as a tradition firmly credited in the parish where it happened:—

> Above a century ago, Siôn Humphries, of this parish, had made his addresses to Ann Thomas, of Creyddyn, on the other side of Conway river. They had made an appointment to meet at a fair in the town of Conway. He, in his way, fell over Pen-maen-mawr; she was over set in the ferry-boat, and was the only person saved out of more than fourscore. They were married, and lived very long together in the parish of Llanvair. She was buried April 11th, 1744, aged 116; he survived her five years, and was buried Dec.

10th, 1749, close by her in the parish church-
yard, where their graves are familiarly shewn
to this day.[4]

The road from hence to Conway is along descent, through which we have a continued scene
of rock and mountain, till within a mile of the
town, when, by a sudden turn to the right, we
gain a view of that, its neighbourhood, and the
most sublime ruin in the kingdom, its magnificent castle. We reached this place at eight o'clock,
and proceeded to the sign of the Bull. At first,
we found some little symptoms of false shame
on entering a respectable inn as *pedestrians*,
but the attention of the people soon convinced
us, we were lowly only in our own eyes; and we
since find they are accustomed to entertain travellers like ourselves, who prefer walking through
this mountainous country to any other mode of
seeing it. Since our arrival here everything has
pleased us. There is one circumstance, indeed,
which immediately puts the traveller in a good
humour with all that he meets with at a Welsh
inn; it is the attendance of *females*, whom, hitherto, we have invariably found as waiters, instead
of men. Exclusive of the pleasure one naturally
feels from the presence of female beauty, there is
also a minute attention and kindness in the manners of women, which give weight to the most
trivial offices they perform for one, and add the

---

4   Pennant's *Wales*, 305.

force of an obligation even to a common act of servitude. The two girls who attend us here, are as beautiful as *Houris*, and by their cheerfulness and simplicity give an additional relish to the dainties spontaneously provided for us by our hospitable landlady.[5]

We were no sooner arrived at our present quarters, than a young man entered our apartment, and requested to know whether we would wish to hear the harp. C—— and I were electrified at the word. Hitherto we had not met with one of these national instruments, and Conway was, of all places, the spot where we should hear its fine tones with best effect. The idea of the ancient bards, who animated the hero to the fight, and eternized his fame by their songs, rushed into our minds;

> *Vos quoque qui fortes animas belloque peremptas*
> *Laudibus in longum vates demittis in ævum,*
> *Plurima securi fudistis carmina bardi.*
> Lucan, *Phar.* i.

And we recollected that the neighbourhood of this place was the scene which a modern poet had chosen for a most sublime description of one of the same important order of men in later times:—

---

5 The ancient Celts, the ancestors of the Welsh, were always attended at their feasts by girls, and boys. Dianovountai ὑπο των νεωτατων παῖδων, ουκ εχονίων ηλικίαν αρρενων τε και Snew.——Diodor. *Sic.* 1. 5.

On a rock, whose haughty brow
Frowns o'er old Conway's foaming flood,
Rob'd in the sable garb of woe,
With haggar'd eye the poet stood;
Loose his beard and hoary hair
Stream'd, like a meteor, to the troubled air;
And with a master's hand, and prophet's fire,
Struck the deep sorrows of his lyre.

GRAY'S *Bard.*

We accordingly expressed a wish to have the harper immediately, and in a few minutes, Mr. Jones, a venerable old man, totally blind, with grey locks, was introduced to us. He proved to be an exquisite player, and did ample justice to his noble instrument, which was the ancient three-stringed Welsh Harp, much better calculated than ours, for expression and effect. It must be allowed that there is a sameness in all the Welsh airs, but though the outline be similar, the features are diversified. An extreme simplicity, and a wild originality, (distinct from the music of other nations) characterize their composition, and the pathetic, which they boast in a high degree, renders them particularly affecting. Mr. Jones gave us a number of traditional bardic tunes, lively and inspiriting, and contrasted them with the plaintive measures of "David of the White Rock," and the solemn dirge-like music of "Morfa Rhuddlan." We regretted that another engagement obliged him to leave us, after playing incessantly for an hour, and affording us a sort of pleasure different from any thing we had hitherto experienced.

Your's, &c.

R. W.

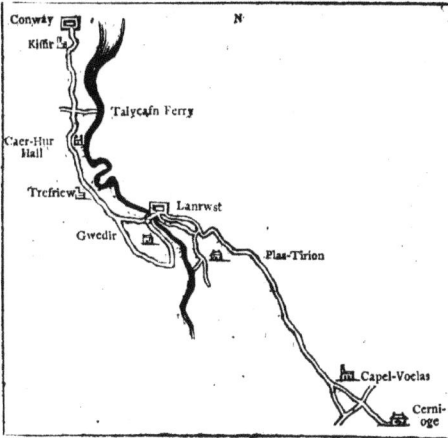

Letter X

TO THE SAME

DEAR SIR, *Coerniog, Aug. 23d.*

ur musical entertainment last night did not cease with the departure of Mr. Jones. We had scarcely dropped into our first sleep, when the sound of the harp, vibrating with the plaintive notes of a solemn composition, pleasingly awaked us. I compared it to an adventure of Ossian.

> In the hall I lay in night. Mine eyes were half closed in sleep. Soft music came to mine ear: it was like the rising breeze, that whirls, at

first, the thistle's beard; then flies, dark shadowy over the grass.

This morning, when we rose, the cause of the serenade was explained to us. On entering our sitting-room we found it occupied by two young gentlemen, who were at breakfast there. We joined the party, and, after some conversation, understood they had engaged Mr. Jones to harp to them after his quitting us, and were so delighted with his performance as to protract it until midnight, which had occasioned the agreeable interruption of our repose. It soon appeared, these gentlemen were, like ourselves, pedestrian travellers, though their route was somewhat different, and their mode of carrying necessary luggage more extravagant than ours. They had left Aberystwyth with an intention of travelling through North-Wales, and proceeding afterwards to the lakes, by the way of Chester and Liverpool; and in order to effect this the more commodiously, had purchased a poney, which carried a portmanteau with their baggage, and was driven before them. So many inconveniences, however, had arisen from this addition to the party, that they resolved to get rid of it, and we left them at Conway in treaty for the sale of the poney, and determined to adopt our method of carrying their necessaries. We walked round Conway before we quitted it, and visited its stupendous castle. The latter was built by Edward I. and comprised the whole of the present town within its yard. I know nothing more striking than the appearance of this fortress from a little distance; the extent and substance of its walls, the number and hugeness of its round towers, erected on a rock, and rising sublimely above a noble estuary, produce an effect prodigiously grand. The exterior walls, which from their thickness seem calculated to endure as long as the rock on which they stand, are about a mile and half in circumference, and express the figure of a Welsh harp, a form chosen, possibly, by Edward in compliment to the newly-conquered Cambrians. The castle itself is of an oblong shape, defended by eight immense projecting towers each having a smaller one issuing from its top. The interior of this is in a state of ruin, but there are sufficient remains to afford a compleat idea of its original plan. Amongst many apartments, the great hall makes the most conspicuous figure. It extends 130 feet in length, 32 in breadth, and is of a proportionate height. On entering this noble room, the idea of ancient revelry instantly occurs to the mind, and imagination hurries back to those times, when it exhibited the splendid scene described by the poet:

> Illumining the vaulted roof,
> A thousand torches flam'd aloof;
> From massy cups, with golden gleam,
> Sparkled the red Metheglin's stream;
> To grace the gorgeous festival,
> Along the lofty-window'd hall,

The storied tapestry was hung:
With minstrelsy the rafters rung
Of harps, that with reflected light
From the proud gallery glitter'd bright:
While gifted bards, a rival throng,
(From distant Mona, nurse of song,
From Teivi, fring'd with umbrage brown,
From Elvy's vale, and Cader's crown,
From many a shaggy precipice
That shades Iërne's hoarse abyss,
And many a sunless solitude
Of Radnor's inmost mountains rude)
To crown the banquet's solemn close,
Themes of British glory chose.

Having surveyed the interior of the castle, we
strolled as far as the rising tide would allow us,
round its outward walls, in order to see a ruined
tower mentioned by Mr. Pennant. It forms, indeed, a scene of devastation well worth a visit.
The rock on which it was built having been excavated for the sake of the stone, the lower part
of the tower gave way, and tumbled in mighty
fragments on the shore beneath; leaving the upper moiety hanging as it were high in air, and
nodding ruin on all who venture to approach it.
Conway itself is but a mean town, with few tolerable houses in it. Another Plas Mawr, or man-
sion-house, occurs here, of similar architecture
with that at Caernarvon, but of earlier date, and
greater extent. It is indeed a vast pile, decorated
within and without in the fantastical fashion of
the time, with ornaments in stone and plaister,

consisting of arms, 'scutcheons, crests, birds, and beasts. The old Greek apophthegm is carved overt he gateway, AvEXY Aπεxy, *bear*, *forbear*, with some Roman letters, and the date of the building 1585.

After wading through a lane-like turnpike road, close and muddy, for a mile and half, we descended into the beautiful vale of Conway, watered by the winding river of that name. On considering the character of this stream, which has nothing "foaming" in it, we were immediately struck with the impropriety of Mr. Grey's epithet for it. The poet, indeed, might have been led into the error by supposing that the Conway resembled the other mountain torrents of Wales, whose course is marked by rage and impetuosity; but had he written from actual observation, he would have known its features are of the opposite kind, and that it meanders in peace and silence through the vale. A scene of great picturesque beauty opens at the village Porthleyd. The road here runs parallel with a chain of rocks on the right, varying their appearance perpetually, from rude, bare crags, to verdant declivities, and lofty eminences crowned with wood. Two cascades enliven the picture on the same side, one pleasingly relieved with shrubs and trees; the other tumbling down a precipice of at least seventy feet in height. To the left, the river is seen following its capricious course through verdant meadows, and beyond it, are mountains sloping down, and gradually uniting with the vale.

The famous rock called *Carreg-y-Gwalch*, the crag of the Falcon, attracted our notice, and we quitted the Llanrwst road, in order to visit it. Various trees, thickly planted, and extremely luxuriant, almost hide it from the eye. The ancient family house of the Gwedir's (now belonging to Lord Gwedir) stands at the foot of the rock, exhibiting a good example of the country residence of a great family in the 16th century, when it was erected. It is now a farm house, and all its pristine glory is extinguished; time was, however, when it made a figure, and boasted a magnificence which no other noble residence in Wales displayed, for tradition asserts, that *Gwedir* was the first house in the principality fitted up with *glass windows*. We proceeded to Llanrwst over a light, beautiful bridge of three arches, built in 1635, designed, as it is said, by Inigo Jones; and from thence cast a "longing lingering look" over the country we had passed, the beautiful vale of Conway, of which we were now to take a parting view. Here we bade adieu to the hills of Snowdon, whose eastern extremities form the precipitous eminences which impend over the road; and to the fine wooded elevations which accompanied us on the opposite side of the river from Conway to the spot where we stood. We quitted the scene with the regret that is felt on separating from a society, in which we have found amusement blended with instruction; in which, whilst the fancy was delighted, the heart was also improved.

Having passed the bridge, we were now in Denbighshire, the river Conway dividing that county from Caernarvonshire. We entered Llanrwst about three o'clock, and surveyed its ancient church and an elegant chapel adjoining it, in both which there are some old tombs and brasses, chiefly commemorating branches of the Wynne family. Quitting the town, we strolled quietly up a long hill towards Capel Voelas, and having attained its summit, caught a beautiful view of a noble vale stretching to the south-west, and bounded, distantly, by the Merioneth mountains. The sun, as if to heighten the contrast between this scene and the country we were shortly to enter, dropped gently from a black cloud by which he had been long hidden, and lighted up with all his splendour the diversified landscape. It was, however, but a transient feast; we soon dipped into a hollow, and pursued a road over barren heaths and dark morasses for ten miles, enlivened by no variety of prospect, nor any one edifice of beauty or curiosity. We arrived at this place at eight o'clock, a solitary inn, in the midst of a desert, chiefly intended for the accommodation of the coaches which run this road. The larder is in unison with the *population* of the country: nothing to be had but a leg of mutton, which, it seems, was tripping over the "dark-brown heath" about three hours ago. We have ordered it to be roasted, tho' we doubt whether a very keen appetite, produced by a fasting walk of twenty-six miles, will render it eatable.

R. W.

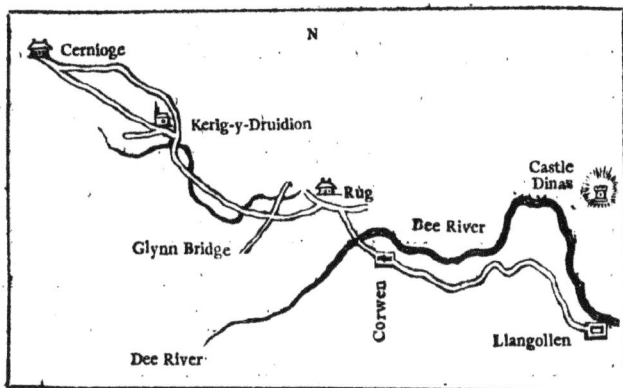

N

Cernioge

Kerig-y-Druidion

Castle
Dinas

Rûg

Dee River

Glynn Bridge

Corwen

Llangollen

Dee River

Letter XI

TO THE SAME

DEAR SIR, *Llangollen, Aug. 24th.*

e have been greatly amused with our day's walk. It has given us a little of everything, of the ridiculous, the beautiful, the solemn; and we have by turns laughed, admired, and moralized, thro' the whole of it. By nine o'clock we had quitted the inn at Cernioge, and were on our road to Kerig-y-Druidion, a village at three miles distance. This place, as its name imports, was connected with the awful superstition of the ancient Britons, and exhibited some years since vestiges of Druidical worship. They are described in a letter given by Camden's *Continuator*, as follows:

> The most remarkable pieces of antiquity in this parish of Kerig-y-Drudion, are those two solitary prisons, which are generally supposed to have been used in the times of the Druids. They are placed about a furlong from each other, and are such huts that each prison can well contain but a single person. One of them is distinguished by the name of Karchar-Kynrik-Rwth, or Kenric-Rwth's prison; but who he was is altogether uncertain. The other is known by no particular title, but that of Kist-vaen, or Stone-Chest, which is common to both, and seems to be a name lately given to them, because they are some what of the form of large chests, from which they chiefly differ in their opening or entrance. They stand north and south, and are each of them composed of seven stones; of these, four, being above six feet long, and about a yard in breadth, are so placed as to resemble the square tunnel of a chimney; a fifth, which is not so long, but of the same breadth, is pitched at the south-end thereof, firmly, to secure that passage. At the north-end is the entrance, where the sixth stone is the lid, and the especial guard of this close confinement. These, and the name of our parish are all the memorials we have of the residence of those ancient philosophers the Druids, &c.[1]

---

1   Camedon, 814.

Of these druidical antiquities there is not now a vestige remaining; they have long since been carried away, and incorporated into a building; and only a recollection of their having formerly stood near the village floats in the minds of some of the cottagers. On reaching this place, we were agreeably surprised to find it thronged with people, true Welsh characters, who were assembled here to celebrate a fair. The sharp features and quick eyes of the men, enlivened by the bargains they were driving, and the round good-humoured faces of the women, animated with the accustomed hilarity and fun of the day, threw a cheerfulness over the scene, that would have stripped spleen herself of the vapours could she have witnessed it. Add to this, my dear sir, the aukward gambols of a merry-andrew, and the strange gabble of a Welsh quack doctor: the grimace of a puppet-shew man, and the bawling of three or four ballad-singers, who chaunted ancient British compositions to different tunes; and, perhaps, your fancy cannot form a scene more ludicrous than Kerig-y-Druidion *fair* exhibited and I felt its force, and not being able to repress our mirth, we indulged it in that noisy manner which invincible risibility produces. But if we were diverted with the whimsical medley before us, the appearance of ourselves was no less an object of ridicule to the honest fair-cousins. The side-pockets of C——, stuffed with specimens and so forth, and my own swollen *spencer*, which, being a compleat novelty in this part of the world, looked like a coat without its skirts, excited extraordinary diversion in the assembly. The grin communicated from face to face, it gradually increased to a giggle, and in a few minutes a general roar of laughter shook the village. We could not but allow the equity of this retaliation; and walked off with an observation similar to that of the traveller who was laughed at in the country of the Guatirs, for not having, like its inhabitants, the ornament of a wen. "Gentlemen, you may consider us as *ridiculous* as you please; but I do assure you, that at *home* we pass for *decent men.*"

Our progress was not checked by anything worth observation, till we reached the seventh mile stone from Cernioge: an hundred yards beyond which, a picture of great magnificence occurs. Here the vale contracts into a deep and narrow glen, fringed with wood on either side; through which the little river Glynn pours its transparent waters. Hitherto this stream has winded quietly and peaceably thro' the valley, but now entering suddenly a bed of disjoined crags, it boils fiercely over them, and rushes between steep, stupendous rocks, (worn, probably, to their present chasm-like state by the force of its waters) till it reaches a lofty arch of simple construction, carried from one side of the fissure to the other. Under this it discharges itself by a fall of many feet into a deep, rocky gulley, so obscured by over-hanging woods, and dark from

its profundity, that the eye cannot trace the torrent through all its madness and horror. The best
point from whence to view this grand *spectacle* is
a little to the south-east of the arch, which is here
seen bestriding the chasm, at the height of one
hundred feet above the water; the rocks beyond,
and the cataract under the bridge, together with
the rising hills and deep shade of lofty woods,
combining finely to compleat the picture.

The walk from hence to Corwen is through a
pleasing, quiet vale, bounded to the right by the
Berwyn mountains. A vast rocky precipice, an
abrupt termination of the lofty Ferwyn, rears
itself above the town to the west, and forms a
singular shelter from the winds of that quarter.
Corwen is a small and neat town, remarkable for
being the spot where Owen Gwynedd, the prince
of North-Wales, assembled his forces in order to
repel the invasion of Henry II. in 1165. The policy
of the Welsh leader, who avoided an engagement,
and weakened the English army by cutting off the
means of supply, was at length successful, and
Henry returned home disgraced and chagrined.
On passing through the town we were struck with
a fierce, gigantic figure, which rose as a sign over
the inn of the place. We found, on enquiry, it was
the representation of Owen Glendower, whose
memory is revered at Corwen, and through the
neighbouring country, which was the scene of his
domestic life, his hospitable mansion standing at
no great distance from the town. Our road to Lla-

ngollen winded at the foot, and along the sides of the Berwyn mountains, through a narrow and beautiful valley, watered by the river Dee, which perpetually varied its character and appearance; sometimes flowing silently along its deepened channel, at others forcing its noisy course over rocks and shelves. Three miles on this side of Llangollen, the landscape becomes unrivalled in point of beauty and variety. The vale of Llan Egwest first catches the attention: a deep and winding valley, terminating in that of Llangollen, shut in by lofty mountains finely wooded, sprinkled with several elegant villas, and enlivened by the tortuous course of the Dee, sporting through it in whimsical meanders. Beyond this are seen the vale of Llangollen with its diversified beauties, the hill of Dinas-Bran rising from it to the height of 1800 feet in the form of a depressed cone,

> Whose dusky brow
> Wears, like a regal diadem, the round
> Of ancient battlements, and ramparts high;
> And frowns upon the vales;

and the Glisseg rocks, a long range of mural precipices, curiously stratified, bounding it to the south. As we descended into the vale, the little town of Llangollen before us, and the remains of Valle-Crucis Abbey, seen partially through their surrounding woods on the left hand, gave additional pleasing features to the picture. The bed of the Dee, also, became truly romantic. It is here composed of dark, laminated slate rocks, the strata of which are disposed in the most whimsical manner; lying in all forms and directions, crossing the current in lofty, oblique ridges, or running parallel with, and horizontal to it. In this manner the river dashes on to the bridge, where, although it has four arches to discharge itself through, yet, preserving its capricious character, it throws its contracted waters down a ledge of many feet deep, and rushes violently through the western one alone.

We arrived at the Hand inn about six o'clock, but finding the whole household busied in preparing dinner for the Margrave of Anspach and his party, we resolved to visit the scenery around Llangollen before we ventured to request any thing for ourselves, as our parsimonious order would have been absorbed and forgotten in an entertainment of two courses and a splendid desert. Having, therefore, secured beds, we set off to contemplate the ruins of Valle-Crucis Abbey and Dinas-Bran Castle.

The former lie at the distance of two miles from Llangollen, a little to the right of the turnpike-road to Ruthin, in a verdant meadow, near the margin of a small brook, and sheltered to the east by lofty hills, whose steep sides are clothed with wood. The vale, though beautiful, is certainly not so picturesque as that of Llangollen; and one naturally feels surprised, that the monks, who generally displayed a good taste in the choice of situation, should have fixed upon one so inferior to the banks of the Dee, which offered themselves at a small distance. I can only account for it, on the supposition, that the roaring of this torrent and the impetuosity of its current might be considered as interruptions to that quiet and abstraction, that silent meditation, in which these secluded ecclesiastics were bound to spend their time, and consequently not calculated to be their immediate neighbour.

The sun was setting when we approached the ruins of Valle-Crucis Abbey, and shed a rich but softened light over the pile; a deep repose reigned around, and not a sound was heard to disturb the reflections which a scene so solemn tended to inspire.

No man, I believe, who is not entirely divested of feeling and taste, can contemplate a religious ruin without sentiments of seriousness and awe. The peculiarities of Gothic architecture are in themselves extremely striking; the pointed termination and light tracery of its figured windows; the variety and number of its niches, recesses, and arches; the elegance of its clustered shafts, and ornamented capitals; and the gloomy perspective of its "long-drawn aisles, "and fretted vaults." The solemn purposes for which the edifice was originally designed, will also naturally occur to the miud, followed by a recollection of the impressive forms of Roman-Catholic worship; its music, torches, and processions; its high masses, and nocturnal rites. But above all, the reflection that we are treading on ground, stored with the dust of the departed, of those who like ourselves were once engaged in the hurry of business, or the pursuits of pleasure, and the conviction that we must shortly be reduced to the same silence and dishonour, will unavoidably combine to produce sentiments of a serious cast, and, for a time at least, abash the insolence of pride, the thoughtlessness of levity, and the effrontery of vice.

The ruins of Valle-Crucis Abbey are well calculated to excite emotions of this nature. The scenery around has the appearance of quiet and retirement, and is sprinkled with little groups of trees, through which the walls of the great abbey church rise in all the beauty of pure Gothic architecture. The area of this building, 180 feet in length, is filled with massive fragments of its fallen roof, and amongst them a number of self-sown shrubs and trees have spontaneously sprung up, throwing an air of additional desolation over the scene. Its style of building, though elegant and tasty, is at the same time perfectly simple. We were struck in particular with the variety and neatness displayed in the capitals of the pillars, and the mouldings of the arches. The east and west ends are the parts best preserved. At the latter, over its large, elegant window, (which is surmounted by a small circular one exquisitely beautiful) runs a line commemorating the person who built or repaired this end; it contains the following letters:—ĀD. ADAM. DMS. Fecit Hoc opus. Pace beata quiescat. Amen. The apartments in which the abbot was lodged, are, in part, remaining, and were converted long since into a farm-house; other offices serve the ignoble purposes of stables, pig-sties, &c.[2]

From hence we proceeded over the fields to Dinas-Bran Hill, which we ascended with considerable toil and some difficulty, as towards the it becomes extremely steep. On the very crown of it are seen the ruins of its ancient castle, and surely never was a better spot chosen for an edifice of this kind. It is well contrasted with the situation of Valle-Crucis Abbey, which the castle overlooks, and formerly protected; and both spots are such as bespeak the original designation of the buildings erected on them; the former for menace and hostility, the latter for meditation and prayer. The prospect from this elevation is grand, diversified, and beautiful, embracing every feature of landscape; mountain and valley, wood and village, river and rock; with the minuter ornaments of neat mansions, and cultivated inclosures. We measured the outward walls, and found them not

---

2   Madocap Griffidd Maylor, prince of Powis, founded a Cistertian Abbey here, about A.D. 1200, and dedicated it to the Blessed Virgin. It was found to be endowed with 1881. 8s. *per annum*, 26th Henry VIII. and was granted 9 Jac. to Edward Wotton. TANNER's *Not. Mon.* 707.

very extensive,[3] but substantial, and impregnably situated, answering the description of the accurate Leland. "The Castelle of Dinas-Brane was never bygge thing, but sette al for strenht as in a place half inaccessible for enemies."[4] The steepness of the hill prevented an easy approach to it on most quarters, and on the south and east, where it was least precipitous, a ditch hollowed out of the solid rock, precluded all access by its breadth and depth. Two wells strongly arched over, and probably of considerable depth, supplied the garrison with water; and the foundations of a chapel evince, that the Lords of Dinas-Bran did not (as is too much the practice in the present day) turn religion out of doors. The castle has been a ruin for upwards of two centuries. Leland found it in that state, when he paid it a visit in the reign of Henry VIII. He mentions a curious particular with respect to its natural history: that an eagle built its nest every year in one of the crags of the mountain, and adds, "The eagle doth sorely assault him that destroith the nest, going doun in one basket, and having another over his hedde to defend the sore stripe of the eagle."[5]

---

3   Eighty-four yards long and fifty broad.

4   Leland, 5 fol. 53.

5   Ib. The amiable authoress of the poem called "Llangollen Vale" has mistaken Mr. Pennant, when she mentions him (in a note) as adducing Leland's testimony, that a pair of eagles built annually in the Glisseg rocks. The naturalist gives the circumstance (according to Leland's account) as belonging to the crags of Dinas-Bran. The interpretation

The origin of Dinas-Bran castle is buried in the remotest antiquity. It may be considered, however, as one of the earliest Welsh castles. Griffith ap Madoc, the arch-traitor, who joined the forces of Henry III. against his country, found a secure refuge in the fortress of Dinas Bran, from the just indignation of the Welsh. After the decease of this chieftain, Edward I. gave the guardianship of his eldest son, a minor, (which, according to the feudal usages, always vested in the prince on the decease of the parent, provided he held a fief of the crown) to John Earl Warren, with a hint, that John would succeed to the estates in case of the minor's decease. It was a dangerous suggestion, and had its intended effect; the poor youth was quickly said to have died, and Earl Warren succeeded to Dinas-Bran as part of the lordship of Yale. A matrimonial alliance passed it afterwards into the family of the Fitzalans, earls of Arundel; where it continued some centuries. It makes at present part of the noble possessions of the Miss Middletons, the co-heiresses of Chirk Castle.

On our return to the Hand inn, we took a passing view of the simple, elegant, and picturesque

---

also of the name of those extraordinary lime-stone rocks (communicated to the lady by a friend) is unfounded and fantastic, made in the true spirit of modern etymology. The word Eglwyseg (even allowing it to be their proper name) has no relation to the Welsh word for an eagle. Creigeau'r Eryri would be the Eagle Rocks, which cannot without the roughest violence be distorted into Eglwyse.

residence of Lady Eleanor Butler and Miss Ponsonby, who had the courage to retire, when in the
meridian of youth and beauty, from the flowery
but fatal paths of fashionable dissipation, and to
dwell with virtue, innocence, and peace, in the
retired shades of Llangollen vale.

Your's, &c.

R. W.

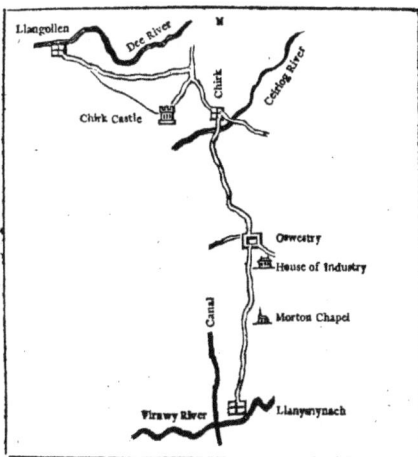

Letter XII

TO THE SAME

Dear Sir,   *Llanywynach, Aug. 25th.*

We have at length left North-Wales, a country which has afforded us the highest gratification. This pleasure, however, arises as much from moral considerations as from natural objects, from the contemplation of the manners and virtues of the people, as of the magnificent scenery amid which they dwell. Of these I shall endeavour to give you a slight sketch; being all, indeed, that our quick progress through the principality allows me to attempt.

On considering the character of the North-Wallians, we find that little variation has taken place in it, during the lapse of 18 centuries; and if we allow for that polish which the progress of society naturally produces on individuals, we shall see the present inhabitant of Merioneth and Caernarvonshire, as well pourtrayed by Diodorus, Cæsar, Strabo, and Livy, as if they had taken the likeness in these days.

The modern, like the ancient Celt, is in person large and robust:[1] his countenance sincere and open, his skin and complexion fair and florid,[2] his eyes blue,[3] and his hair of a yellowish tinge.[4] As he thus nearly resembles his great ancestor inperson, he is also equally like him in mind and disposition. Openness and candour are prominent features in the Welsh character of the present day; they were full as strikingly displayed by the ancient Celtic nations.[5] Their hospitality you are enabled to judge of, from the examples of it which I have mentioned in the preceding letters;

---

1 Οι δε ανδρες ευμήκεςεροι των Κελτων εισι.—Strabo, lib. iv. "The men (Britons) are the tallest of the Celts."

2 Fusa et candida corpora.—Tit. Liv. lib. xxxviii.

3 Germani truces et coerulei oculi.—Tacit. de Mor. Germ. sect. 4.

4 Ταις δε κομαις εκφύσεως ξανθοι.—Diod. Sic. lib. v. "Profusely covered with yellow hair."

5 Τοῖς δὲ ἤθεσιν ἁπλοῦς εἶναι, καὶ πολὺ κεχωρισμένους τῆς τῶν ἀνθρώπων ἀγχινοίας καὶ πονηρίας.—Diod. Sic. lib. v. "They are simple in their manners, and very distant from the cunning and wickedness of modern days."

amongst the ancients they were highly extolled for the same amiable quality.[6] That quickness of feeling, so apparent in the Welsh, which frequently displays itself in fierce, but transient fits of passion, and as often produces quarrels and bloodshed, perpetually embroiled the Celts in war and slaughter.[7] National pride, a venial defect in the character of a people, since it arises only from the excess of laudable affections, is proverbial amongst the inhabitants of the principality, and they seem to have it by hereditary descent from their Celtic forefathers, who thought more highly of themselves, than the polished nations around them conceived they had a right to do.[8]

I have before observed, that a religious spirit prevails amongst the lower orders of the Welsh, which produces a characteristic decency of manners in that description of people. It is, however, much tinged with superstition, and the belief in spirits and apparitions is very general. The names of many mountains and rocks evince, that they are considered as the residences of subordinate intelligences;[9] and this is accounted for,

---

6 *Mortalium omnium erga hospites humanissimi.*— Procop.

7 Εισι δεμαχιμωτατοι.—Herodian. l. iii. "They are prone to battle."

8 *Celtæ magna de seipsis sentiunt.*

9 Similar superstitions were found amongst the ancient Celts. "*Complures genios colunt. Aereos, terrestres, et alia minora dæmonia, quæ in aquis fontium et fluminûm versari dicuntur.*" Procop. *de Goth.* lib. ii.

not so much, perhaps, from the credulity natural to ignorant people, as from the circumstances of the scenery wherein they reside, the gloom and desolation of which, added to its being liable to singular and striking variations in appearance, have a strong tendency to affect the human mind (naturally timid) with superstitious fears and whimsical notions. Similar situations will produce similar manners; and hence it happens that their brethren of the Scotch Highlands entertain the same opinions, in this respect, with the inhabitants of Wales. The ghosts of the departed, and the spirits of the mountains, rocks, and winds, make a conspicuous figure in the poetry of the North; and some of the sublimest passages of Ossian have their origin in these, popular prejudices:—

> Fillan is like a spirit of heaven, that descends from the skirt of winds. The troubled ocean feels his steps, as he strides from wave to wave. His path kindles before him. Islands shake their heads on the heaving seas.
>
> How dreary is the night! The moon is darkened in the sky; red are the paths of ghosts, along its sullen face! Dull is the roaring of streams from the valley of dim forms. I hear thee, spirit of my father, on the eddying course of the wind. I hear thee, but thou bendest not forward thy tall form from the skirts of night.

These notions are, probably, unfounded, but they are not uninteresting, nor do we feel ourselves inclined to reprobate the mild superstition in which they originate. It is a principle that arises from the feelings and affections of nature; and is, at all events, more amiable, than the cold philosophism of the present day, which disbelieves every thing, which contracts and petrifies the heart, deadens the affections, and destroys all the finer sensibilites of the soul.

The Welsh females still retain that beauty of face, which drew encomiums on their Celtic mothers, from the writers of antiquity.[10] They are middle-sized, and well shaped, strikingly modelled according to the taste of Anacreon.[11] Their eyes are dark and sparkling, and their complexion and teeth fair and white. Though their persons display a proper degree of symmetry, yet they are obviously stouter than the women of South-England, and inherit a great portion of that strength which Diodorus mentions as characterizing the Celtic females.[12] Till within these few years a compleat specimen of this hardy race remained, who inhabited a cottage on the borders of Llanberris lake. Mr. Pennant gives the following entertaining account of her:—

---

10 *Γυναίκας εχέσιν ευειδείς.*—Diod. Sic. I. v. "They have beautiful women, or wives."

11 *Λυρίζων*
Παρα σοις, Διονυσε, σήκοις,
Μελα χςρης βαθυκολπο,
      — χορεύσω. ΩΔ. i.

12 *Sic. ut sup.*

This was *Margaret uch Evan*, of Penllyn, the greatest hunter, shooter, and fisher of her time. She kept a dozen at least of dogs, terriers, greyhounds, and spaniels, all excellent in their kinds. She killed more foxes in one year than all the confederate hunts do in ten; rowed stoutly, and was queen of the lake; fiddled excellently, and knew all our old music; did not neglect the mechanic arts, for she was a very good joiner; and notwithstanding she was 70 years of age, was the best wrestler of the age, and few young men dared to try a fall with her. Some years ago she had a maid of congenial qualities; but death, that mighty hunter, at last earthed this faithful companion of hers.[13]

The dress of the Welsh women is exactly similar throughout the principality, and consists of these particulars: a petticoat of flannel, the manufacture of the country, either blue or striped; a kind of bed-gown with loose sleeves, of the same stuff, but generally of a brown colour; a broad handkerchief over the neck and shoulders; a neat mob-cap, and a man's beaver hat. In dirty, or cold weather, the person is wrapped in along blue cloak, which descends below the knee. Except when particularly dressed, they go without shoe or stocking; and even if they have these luxuries, the latter in general has no foot to it. The man's attire is a jacket, waistcoat, and breech-

---

13   Snowdonia, 158.

es, of their country flannel, the last of which are
open at the knees, and the stockings (for the men
generally wear them) are bound under the knees
with red garters. Both men and women are vi-
vacious, cheerful, and intelligent, not exhibiting
that appearance of torpor and dejection which
characterize the labouring poor of our own country; their wants being few, are easily supplied; a
little milk, which their own mountain goat, or the
benevolence of a neighbouring farmer, affords
them, an oaten cake, and a few potatoes, furnish
the only meal which they desire. Unvitiated by
communication with polished life, they continue to think and act as nature dictates. Confined
to their own mountains, they witness no scenes
of profusion and extravagance to excite envy or
malignity, by a comparison between their own
penury and the abundance of others. They look
round and see nothing but active industry and
unrepining poverty, and are content.

> Tho' poor the peasant's hut, his feasts tho' small,
> He sees his little lot, the lot of all;
> Sees no contiguous palace rear its head
> To shame the meanness of his humble shed;
> No costly lord the sumptuous banquet deal,
> To make him loath his vegetable meal;
> But calm, and bred in ignorance and toil,
> Each wish contracting, fits him for the soil.

We surveyed the church of Llangollen, before
our departure from the town, and were some-

what struck with the name of the venerable saint to whom it is dedicated, which in itself forms a little nomenclature. It is as follows: *Yrth St. Collen ap Gwynnawg ap Clydawg ap Cowrda ap Caradog Freichfras ap Lleyr Merim ap Einion ap Cunedda Wledig*; the sexton repeated it twice or thrice, with emphasis and deliberation, but it is to Mr. Pennant that I am indebted for the orthography of this pompous genealogical title.

Shortly before we reached the three-mile stone, an object of considerable curiosity and importance led us from the turnpike-road, about half a mile to the left hand, to a place called Pont-y-Swlty. The Dee, which has here assumed a quieter character than it displays at Llangollen, flows through a rich and beautiful valley. Across this stream, [at right angles with it] the canal, running from Shrewsbury to Chester, is intended to be carried, by means of an aqueduct of stupendous design and most laborious execution. The aqueduct itself will be of cast-iron, and supported by stone pillars, three of which (for they are nearly constructed) stand in the bed of the river. These are ten feet in breadth, by five feet in depth, at the base, and eight feet by four at the top; and rise 120 feet above the bed of the river. The expence of this vast work, it is imagined, will amount to 50,000l.; a striking example of the wealth and spirit of individuals in this country, who, under the peculiar pressure of the present times, have courage to suggest, and ability to execute, a plan so grand and expensive. Returning from the river, and passing over a hill which is nothing less than a mighty mass of rich and productive limestone, we crossed into the *old* Oswestry road, and continued in it till we reached a farm called Vrond farm. In a field belonging to this estate, and immediately adjoining to the turnpike-road, is a knoll, or elevation, commanding a prospect wonderfully extensive and diversified; the vale of Llangollen, and its surrounding mountains, the hills of Cheshire and Shropshire, the mazy windings of the Dee, and the rich country through which it flows; the noble mansions, Chirk Castle and Wynne-Stay; many other elegant seats, and a large portion of thirteen different counties. We now quitted the turnpike-road, and bent our course towards Chirk Castle thro' the park, an extensive undulating tract of ground, adorned with noble plantations, scattered over it in a tasty and judicious manner. The situation of the mansion is very happy. It stands on the brow of a noble hill, exhibiting a view that stretches into 17 counties. There is something extremely august and solemn in the building itself, turreted at the top, and strenghtened with tower bastions on every side; and when we consider that it has stood since the time of Edward I. and braved the devastation and revolutions of five centuries, it will appear to be one of the most venerable, as well as perfect castellated mansions in the kingdom. The Lords of Dinas-Bran numbered Chirk amongst their other possessions until the conclusion of the 13thcentury, when the two sons of Griffidd ap Madog (the last of that race) were placed by the king under the guardianship of two of his barons, Earl Warren and Roger Mortimer. I observed to you before, that Warren fulfilled his duty by murdering his charge, and was rewarded for the atrocious act with the demesne of Yale. Roger Mortimer acted the same bloody part by his unfortunate ward, and received from the hands of his master the manors of Chirk and Nan-hendwy. Mortimer built the present castle, though much of it has been re-edified since his time, one of its sides and three towers being destroyed by Lambert, when it was delivered into his hands during the civil wars of the last century. This noble mansion, with the extensive territory attached to it, has been in the possession of the Middleton family since the year 1614. It lately vested in two of the Miss Middletons, by the demise of their brother, who died some few months since. Leaving Chirk Castle, we wandered through its park and inclosures to the village of that name, from which descending into a beautiful vale, we crossed the Ceiriog by a noble modern bridge of one arch, and simple but elegant construction. Here we were astonished by another wonderful instance of the effects of human labour. Along the hill on the south-eastern side of the river runs the canal before-mentioned, and to convey its waters across the valley and over the river, a prodigious aqueduct between fifty and sixty feet above the level of the water, and several hundred yards in length, is now constructing.[14] All here is bustle and business; in one spot are seen numerous parties of workmen driving on the course of the canal in spite of rock, mountain, and every other obstacle which nature has thrown in their way. At a little distance the builders of the aqueduct are employed in their stupendous labour. And immediately upon the canal several miners perforate the mountain, and follow up a rich vein of coal lately discovered, which, from its happy situation, must prove the certain source of future fortune. Quitting this scene, we passed through the ancient town of Oswestry, a place famed in Saxon history and Monkish tales. Here Oswald, the Christian king of the Northumbrians, was slain in battle by Penda, the Pagan prince of Mercia; and being afterwards canonized by the ecclesiastics, to whom he had been a devoted friend during life, it was here also that miracles were performed by his reliques on the diseased bodies of man and beast. A well, which formerly possessed many sanative powers, and in the times of papacy drew numberless of the disordered to its healing spring, may still be seen. Its miraculous qualities, however, have long since ceased, but we found it wonderfully effica-

---

14 Pontcysyllte Aqueduct, which was completed in 1805. —Ed.

cious in slaking a feverish thirst, occasioned by a long walk and intense heat. Our road to Lla-nymynach, which we reached at 8 o'clock, lay through a very different country to what we had been accustomed to for the last ten days. We now found a soil rich and productive, scientific husbandry, large-sized cattle, weighty crops, and industrious labour in all its forms. The change was agreeable, and excited pleasurable emotions, almost equal in degree, tho' different in kind, to those which we had experienced in surveying the scenery of Merioneth and Caer-narvonshire. Nature in her magnificence, her wonders, and her horrors, was then the subject of our contemplation; human art and industry, with their ingenious exertions, and beautiful effects, now claim our attention. Each, however, affords gratification to the mind, and gives rise to appropriate reflections. In the former scenes, "we look through nature up to nature's God;" the sublimity of the objects before us fills our souls with sentiments of wonder and adoration, and our thoughts glance from earth to heaven. In the latter, we contemplate with astonishment the fertile invention, the ingenious contrivance, and the unconquerable perseverance of man, who makes nature herself subservient to his use; and converts the rocks and mountains, the woods, the winds, and waves, into means of comfort, wealth, and happiness! The excellence of his nature, and the extent of his talents, rise in our estimation, in proportion as we attend to his works; and we feel a conscious dignity in reflecting, that Providence has placed ourselves in so exalted a rank in the scale of his creatures.

Your's, &c.

R. W.

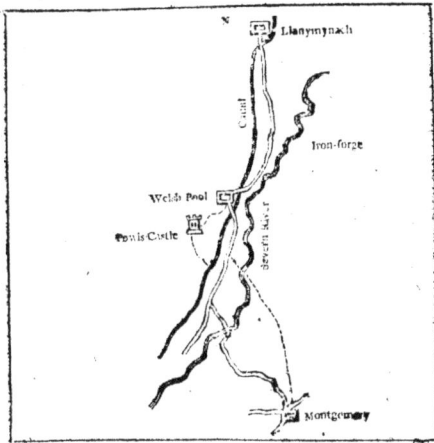

Letter XIII

TO THE SAME

DEAR SIR, *Montgomery, Aug. 26th.*

ur first object this morning was Llanymynach hill, which we had been
prevented from surveying last night
by our late arrival at the inn. We
accordingly rose at six o'clock, and
ascended it before breakfast.

Llanymynach hill is a vast rock of calcareous
marble, fit either for the work of the mason, or
to be burned into lime. It is of great length, and
runs nearly north and south, the extremities terminating in abrupt precipices. In our way to its

summit, we crossed a British work consisting of a stone rampart and three fosses. We passed also some of the lime-kilns, of which there is a very great number, belonging to Lord Bradford, constantly burning lime for manure, to supply avast and perpetual sale. It is considered as the best in that part of the kingdom for the farmer's purposes, who carries it to the distance of twenty miles. At the kilns the price of the best lime is 7d. per bushel, and of the worst 6d. The labourers employed in burning it, make on an average in summer 16d. per day, in winter 12d. Here also we were shewn the vestiges of Roman labour; a very considerable excavation of the mountain, with many small pits, in shape like inverted cones. These were formed by the sagacious and industrious conquerors of the world in search of the copper, lead, and calamine, with which Lla-nymynach hill abounds. No speculation of this kind has been attempted of late years, though it appears to be very likely, from the presence of mineral in every part of the mountain, that a trial now would be as successful as it was formerly. Our pains in adding to the walk of to-day, and ascending Llanymynach, were amply repaid by these objects of curiosity, and the noble prospect that opened to us from the summit of it. We here caught a full and parting view of the plain of Sa-lop; the rich and undulating vale of the Severn, watered by its majestic river; the Breddin hills, and the dark top of the Ferwyn mountains. The irresistible demands of appetite compelled us, at length, to return to breakfast at our inn, where everything excellent in its kind awaited our arrival, particularly a delicate light kind of bread (somewhat like the French rolls) which we observe the people of these parts have the art of making superior to any we ever before tasted. We quitted Llanymynach at ten o'clock, and took the side of the canal (a branch of the Ellesmere) to Welsh-Pool, which only increased the distance one mile, and relieved us from floundering through a Shropshire turnpike-road, of all public ways the most abominable. This observation, however, may perhaps only apply to the part of the country through which we have passed, where, in addition to a deep soil, and a scarcity of materials for reparation, incalculable injury arises to the roads from the constant carriage of coals to Llanymynach hill, and of limestone from it. As we skirted the canal, the scene was enlivened by barges passing and repassing, contrasted with the busy operations of harvest on its banks. Here we observed a good systematical husbandry, exerted on a fine loamy soil, producing upon the average three quarters per acre. It concerned us, however, to understand, that the canals, though highly advantageous in a national point of view, were very detrimental to the individuals through whose property they passed. The banks which confine them can never be constructed with a sufficient compactness and solidity to prevent the water from oozing through them; the consequence is, the adjoining grounds are chilled by an undue degree of moisture, the grass is soured, or the grain destroyed.

Two miles from Llanymynach we were conveyed over the river Vyrnwy, by means of another aqueduct, admirably constructed, of vast strength and stability. From hence to Welsh Pool nothing particularly striking occurs, till within a short distance of that town, when the Breddin hills to the left, and the magnificent seat of Earl Powis, with its well-wooded, undulating grounds rising to the south, form a pleasing picture. The assizes being held at Welsh Pool this week, we thought it best to hasten through the place with all possible expedition; for to declare the honest truth, a walk of 400 miles, for the most part over rocks and mountains, has rendered our appearance so suspicious, as to excite some fears in us of apprehension under the vagrant act. Welsh-Pool, indeed, holds out nothing to detain the traveller; it is an ill-built straggling town, remarkable only for being the storehouse of the flannel manufactured in the upper counties, which are brought down here, and disposed of to the wholesale dealers who frequent the place. Striking into the fields, we followed a path that led us to the park of Powis Castle, which stands about a mile to the right of the Montgomery turnpike-road. Its situation is elevated and commanding, looking over a vast tract of country, the greatest part of which was formerly subject to its lords. The entrance is august, between two tower bastions, and the whole building brings to the recollection the cumbersome magnificence, and tastless splendour of former days. In front, two immense terraces one above another form the ascent to the house; ornamented with vases, statues, &c. All here is in the style of the last century, and the description of Timon's villa is realized:

> Lo, what huge heaps of littleness around!
> The whole a labour'd quarry above ground;
> Two cupids squirt before: a lake behind
> Improves the keenness of the northern wind.
> His gardens next your admiration call,
> On every side you look, behold the wall!
> No pleasing intricacies intervene,
> No artful wildness to perplex the scene;
> Grove nods at grove, each alley has a brother,
> And half the platform just reflects the other,

The recorded history of this castle commences early in the 12th century, when it was founded by Cadwgan ap Bleddyn ap Cynvyn. In the conclusion of the same century, Herbert archbishop of Canterbury[1] besieged and took it, and added to its strength by new fortifications and a powerful garrison. These, however, were insufficient to resist the attacks of Gwenwynwyn its former lord, who again reduced it shortly after its surrender to Herbert. In his successors it continued for some

---

1   Hubert Walter (1160 - 1205). —Ed.

generations, and afterwards passed into the family of the Charltons in Shropshire. Queen Elizabeth sold it to Sir William Herbert second Earl of Pembroke,[2] who being created Lord Powys, became ancestor to the Marquisses of Powys, During the civil wars it fell into the hands of Sir Thomas Middleton, who pillaged the castle, and made its lord a prisoner. George Earl of Powys possesses this noble demesne at present, which now consists of seventeen manors.[3] The afternoon becoming hazy and uncomfortable, we took a shorter road to Montgomery than the turnpike, and passing the Severn at a ferry where preparations are making for the erection of a bridge, we hastened to the place of our destination, which we reached at six o'clock. Montgomery is most agreeably situated on the declivity of a hill, rising to a considerable height behind it, and was formerly defended by a noble castle, strongly seated on a lofty and romantic rock,the ruins of which have a very picturesque effect from a little distance. Originally part of the possessions of Baldwyn, the friend and companion of William the Conqueror, it is probable he became the founder of the castle, as its small remains display some peculiarities of Norman architecture.

---

2 Sir Edward Herbert (1544 - 1595) purchased it from Edward Grey, the illegitimate son of Edward Grey, 3rd Baron of Powis. William Herbert, 1st Baron Powis (1573 - 1655) was born in the castle. —Ed.

3 Pennant, 379.

It afterwards came into the powerful family of Mortimer, and continued there till the death of Edmund Earl of March. During the disturbances of the last century, being taken by Sir Thomas Middleton the Oliverian, it underwent the fate of numberless other edifices of the same kind, was dismantled by order of the parliament, and reduced to the melancholy heap of ruins which it now exhibits.

Your's, &c.

R. W.

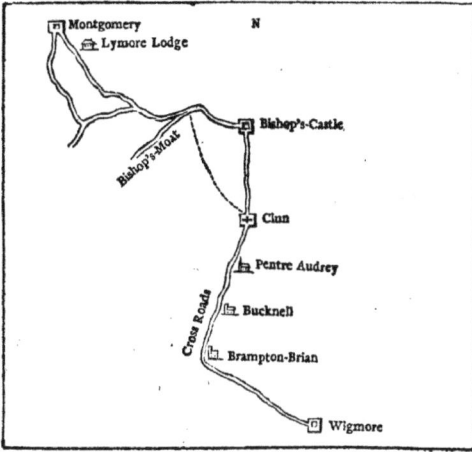

Letter XIV

TO THE SAME

DEAR SIR,   *Wigmore, Aug. 27th.*

inding that the term of our intended absence from home would allow
the extension of our tour beyond
the limits originally proposed to
it, we this morning agreed to cross
over to Hereford, and traverse the banks of the
Wye from thence to Chepstow, instead of di-
recting our steps immediately to the New Passage. Having attended service, therefore, at the
church of Montgomery, we left that town at half
past twelve, on our road to Clun. After a walk

of five miles, a long ascent conducted us to the summit of Castle-Rising hill, from whence we enjoyed a noble view of the country which we had traversed during the last two days; the hills of Salop, and the rich vale of Montgomery. Here, also, we overlooked the town of Bishop's Castle; Walcot, the noble seat of Lord Clive, and its adjoining grounds; together with a considerable part of Herefordshire. Leaving the direct road, we struck across the downs to Clun, and amused ourselves for a few minutes in contemplating its ruined castle and fallen grandeur. Originally built by Fitzalan,[1] (descended from the noble Norman of that name, who founded the Arundel family) Clun castle was the strong fortress from whence the Lords Marchers rushed into the adjoining territories of the Welsh princes, pillaged and laid waste the unsuspecting country, and to which they afterwards retreated with their prisoners and spoil. It paid the penalty of its lawless system long since, being a ruin in the time of Leland, who only mentions it as having been "bothe stronge and well builded;" it has, now,

> No honourable note,
> No chronicle of all its warlike pride
> To testify what once it was, how great,
> How glorious, and how fear'd. So perish all,

---

1   William Fitzalan did not establish Clun Castle; he obtained it by marriage to Isabelle de Say (1132 - 1199), daughter of Helias (d. 1165), son of Henry, son of Robert (d. 1098), who was the founder of the structure. —Ed.

Who seek their greatness in dominion held of war;
Over their fellows, or the pomp
And be as thou forgotten, and their fame
Cancell'd like thine.

On enquiring our road to Wigmore, where we
proposed passing the evening, we were pleased
to understand it was so plain and direct as not to
be mistaken; and more over, that the distance of
seven short miles would lead us to our place of
destination. We had often had occasion in Wales
to observe the inaccuracy of the common people's ideas with respect to distance, and generally
found the addition of half a mile to the real meas-
urement necessary to form a Welsh mile. But in
Shropshire they seem to be still more ignorant
in this respect, for upon a calculation of the time
expended in walking from Clun to Wigmore,
and of the speed which we used in the journey,
we estimated, with the utmost fairness, that we
had passed over at least twelve miles of country.
This indeed received the confirmation of a third
person. We had not proceeded more than three
miles upon this remarkably plain and easy road,
before we were utterly at a loss how to proceed,
from the intricacies of a hilly country, covered
with cross-roads and paths that intersected each
other, and offered themselves in every direction. Fortunately, a solitary horseman, who was
travelling to the town of Presteign, appeared at
this juncture, and relieved us from our state of
perplexity, by pointing out the road we should

pursue; you will, however, imagine our chagrin, when he observed, in addition to his information, that even if we threaded the mazes of the route to Wigmore, we should find that we had at least nine miles further to walk. He certainly neither overrated the distance or the difficulties, for after all our enquiries and minute observation of the directions afforded us, I am confident we should have wandered about the open downs of the hills, or floundered through the narrow dirty lanes of the vales, till this time, had we not met with an honest hind who lived near the place to which we were going, and kindly offered to conduct us thither.

Under his convoy we pursued our walk with fresh spirit, and reached the ancient village of Brampton-Brian in sufficient time to survey the old and singular little church there. Its peculiarity consists in one end of it being attached to the keep of a ruined castle. This fragment is the only remain of a fortress built in the early Norman times, by Brian de Brampton, the head of an ancient and powerful family of that name, from whom the village also received its appellation. The fief of Brampton continued to be held in an uninterrupted succession till the reign of Edward II. by the lords of this family, when it passed into that of the Harleys, (ancestors of the present Lord Oxford) by the marriage of Robert Harley with Margaret daughter and co-heir of Brian de Brampton. Here it has continued ever since, and now makes part of the large estates of the Earl of Oxford. This nobleman has still a mansion in the village, capable of being converted into a desirable residence. The dilapidated state of the building, however, and the wild appearance of its extensive garden, evince that it has not been hitherto honoured with much of his lordship's attention. The former consequence of Brampton-Brian would perhaps have been in sufficient to have preserved its name from oblivion, had not a wag, in the early part of this century, contributed, by a piece of humour, to keep it floating in the recollection of the world. This was Harry Hall, the organist of Hereford, of facetious memory. The owner of Brampton Brian, a starched puritanical character, having excited the resentment of our poet, he determined to be revenged by making him the subject of his wicked wit. An opportunity soon offered: a female domestic was found to be in that situation which is honourable only in a married dame. This discovery produced considerable confusion in the family at the manor house; the credulous and unfortunate girl was turned out of doors with every mark of ignominy, harshness, and cruelty; lustrations were performed, and the walls resounded with anathemas against the wretch whose levities had polluted the hitherto immaculate residence of this disciple of old John Knox. Hall heard of the circumstance, and immediately wrote a well-known song on the subject; which, though rather a loose composition, is not devoid of wit; the versification is smooth, the points are good, and the epigrammatic turn at the conclusion is sufficiently neat.

The rain now began to fall in heavy drops; we therefore hastened on to Wigmore, through miserable roads, and reached the Castle inn, the public-house of the village, wet, dirty, and tired, at eight o'clock. The looks of our landlord, who opened the door to us, afforded us no favourable idea of the welcome we should receive. In truth, we soon discovered we were not to expect very hospitable treatment. To our questions, whether we could be provided with supper and beds, a sullen no was returned by the deep voice of the host, which the shrill pipe of his wife (who spoke from the kitchen) very audibly confirmed. After a parley, however, of some length, in which we described our situation and fatigue, together with the impracticability of our proceeding further to-night, we gained admission into an ordinary parlour, as well as an unwilling promise that something should be provided for our refreshment. We now found that our appearance and mode of travelling had excited suspicions no way favourable to our honesty; for scarcely had we seated ourselves by the fire, when a maid, entering the room, proceeded to a corner-cupboard, and slyly conveying into her apron three or four silver spoons, and a small silver cup which had hitherto formed the splendid ornaments of the parlour, removed them from a situation in which our host and his wife evidently conceived it was dangerous to allow the family plate to remain. Notwithstanding this proof of their want of confidence, I was not without hopes of bringing them to their accustomed cordiality; nor have I been disappointed in my endeavour. Oh! courtesy, how wonderful is thy power. Thy gentle influence stealing softly to the heart, smooths every asperity, subdues each unkindly emotion, and by a gradual metamorphosis, changes the gloom of sullenness into the smile of complacency. The curled brow of our landlord at length relaxed, and assumed its wonted serenity; his wife also became less peevish and ill-natured; we have gotten an excellent supper, and are provided with two comfortable, well-aired beds.

Your's, &c.

R. W.

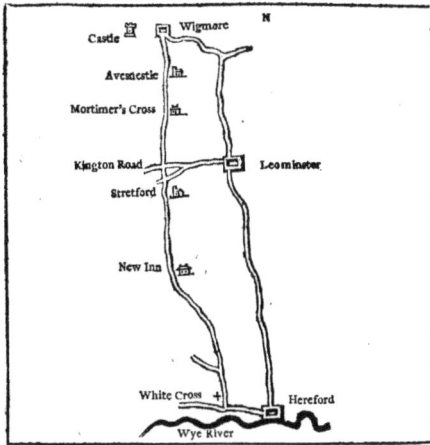

Letter XV

TO THE SAME

DEAR SIR,   *Hereford, Aug. 28th.*

The noble remains of Wigmore Castle claimed our attention very early this morning. They stand to the west of the town, on a natural hill of considerable elevation, and form a very picturesque ruin. An artificial mount was raised to receive the keep, which rises greatly higher than the outward walls, and produces, at a short distance, a grand effect. The chief entrance is to the east, and strikes the eye as being singularly low; a profuse mantle of ivy crowns its summit, which creeping also over some of the adjoining bastions, gives an air of venerable majesty to the mouldering pile. Wigmore Castle was built by William Earl of Hereford; it afterwards came into the Mortimer family, the heads of which lived here for some centuries in almost princely grandeur; extending their jurisdiction over all the surrounding country, exercising many of the rights of sovereignty, holding their own courts, and trying and executing the criminals found within their demesne. It is now an appendage to the estate of Lord Oxford, his ancestors having enjoyed it ever since the reign of James I. who granted it to Thomas Harley, esq; of Brampton Brian, the great grandfather of the Lord Treasurer in Queen Anne's reign. In our way from the castle we surveyed the church of Wigmore; a spacious, ancient edifice, and particularly curious from the circumstance of its being chiefly constructed of large blocks of composition, (formed in moulds) light and porous, and in appearance very much resembling the volcanic production called pumice-stone. The most striking object within the church, is a sumptuous seat, facing the pulpit. It is fitted up with every accommodation of ease, and refinement of luxury; an elegant Buzaglo stove, a handsome figured carpet, half a dozen fashionable chairs, and a most splendid crimson velvet curtain, adorning, with its fantastic festoons, the plain arch in front of the pew. We could not but view this violation of the simplicity so proper to be observed in the style of accommodations in place of public worship, with considerable disgust. The lightsome decorations of a modern drawing-room assimilate but aukwardly with the solemnity of a Gothic pile; and the motives that suggest this ostentatious display of superior wealth, within walls where pride should never enter, are far from being congenial with those sentiments and affections which the house of GOD is calculated to inspire. The church-yard afforded us a view of the flat unwholsome country to the north of the village, which is flooded during all the winter months, and breathes rheums and agues. From hence also we saw, about a mile to the left, the grange of the noble Abbey of Wigmore, founded originally by Sir Hugh de Mortimer, and finally settled here in the year 1179. The monks were of the order of St. Austin, and enjoyed, from the bounty of the founder alone, estates amounting, at the dissolution, to upwards of 300l. *per annum*. On the right, our attention was directed to a solitary farm-house called the government, where the steward of the castle was wont to reside, who received from the numerous tenants of the barony, the rents of their respective farms in kind, (according to the usual mode of tenure in the feudal times) and supplied the castle with the means of that hospitality which it formerly exhibited.

The violent rains that had fallen in the night rendered our walk extremely uncomfortable.

Every step plunged us ancle-deep in mud; nor was our labour at all recompensed by interesting scenery, or amusing occurrence. The only place we passed connected with remarkable circumstance was Mortimer's Cross, a public house three miles from Wigmore, near the intersection of two cross-roads, in the immediate neighbourhood of which, one of the bloody contests fought between the houses of York and Lancester was decided. Here Mortimer, the young earl of March and baron of Wigmore, on the eve of Candlemas-day, in the year 1461, attacked and discomfited an army of the Lancastrians, led by Gaspar Tudor earl of Pembroke, and James Butler earl of Ormond. The battle was fought in a large field near the Ludlow road called King's-land, and 3800 of Margaret's followers were added to the bloody list of those already slain in this precious dispute. Having reached Hereford, we called on our friend Mr. Wathen, whose active attention and promptness to oblige are experienced and acknowledged by all who have the pleasure of his acquaintance. On him we depended for directions in our expedition down the Wye, and his usual kindness has been displayed in making out for us a minute delineation of the course of the river, its most picturesque points, and the objects of curiosity in the neighbourhood of its banks. Nor is this all: he has promised to meet us at Wilton-bridge near Ross, on Wednesday morning, and to be our guide from thence to the beautiful scenery around Tintern Abbey.

Your's, &c.

R. W.

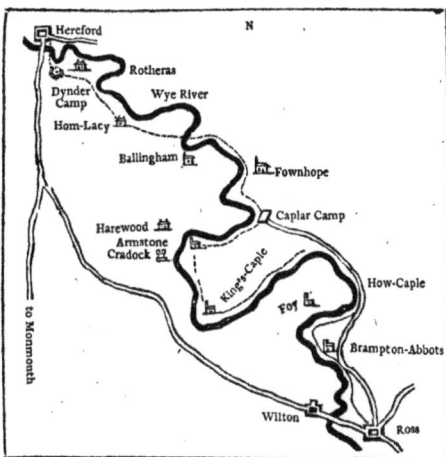

Letter XVI

TO THE SAME

DEAR SIR,   *Wilton-Bridge, Aug. 29th.*

forbear to make any remarks on the city of Hereford, as much has already been done towards its illustration; and as ample accounts of it are scattered through books which you have frequent opportunities of turning over. The Wye alone will employ my attention. Let me observe then, in the first place, that there is no mode of seeing its numerous and varied beauties so satisfactorily, as that of following its sinuosities on foot. The usual practice, you know, is to

189

go from Hereford to Ross in a carriage, and from thence drop down the river to Chepstow in a boat, a voyage performed in two days. By these means, however, all the beautiful scenery between Hereford and Ross is omitted, the expence of the expedition is enhanced in the proportion of six to one, and several fine views of the river from its neighbouring elevations are entirely lost.

Under the direction of Mr. Wathen, who added to his other favours that of accompanying us the first three miles of this day's walk, we crossed the Wye at Castle-Green, and struck through the grounds and farm-yard of Rotherwas, the elegant family mansion of Charles Bodenham, esq. Dyndor hill lay before us, and the Roman encampment, which receives its name from it, on our left hand. From hence we took a farewell view of Hereford and its neighbourhood, the adjoining hills, and the black mountain, that striking boundary to the north-west, and commanded a diversified and sweeping prospect to the opposite point. Our approach to Hom-Lacy, was by a gradual descent of nearly a mile, through a rich, productive country, glittering with a heavy crop of ripening corn. This substantial mansion is one of the many houses belonging to his Grace the Duke of Norfolk. The older part of it displays the aukward style of Elizabeth's time; the later was built towards the beginning of the present century. Its situation is in the taste of the age when it was constructed; quiet and retired, commanding a beautiful but confined view from the front. This was the situation which our forefathers affected; their shyness induced them to ambush their country seats in woods and bottoms, and they are, perhaps, on this account more interesting than modern rural residences, which (as has been well observed) disclose all their glories at once, and never excite expectation by concealment, by gradual approaches, and by interrupted appearances. Hom-Lacy was for some centuries in the ancient family of the Scudamores, whose ancestor, Saint Scudamore, (so called from the *scutum amoris divini*, which he took for his arms) attended William the Conqueror, in his expedition to England. A descendant of his, Philip de Scudamore, in the 14th century, settled at Hom-Lacy, which continued to be the principal seat of the family till the year 1716, when the last Viscount Scudamore dying, the estate vested in his only child, a daughter. By Charles Fitzroy, esq; (her second husband) she also had a daughter, to whom the property descended. This lady married the present Duke of Norfolk in 1771, and added Hom-Lacy to the princely domains of that nobleman. It was in this pleasing retreat that our admirable poet, Mr. Pope, frequently wooed the muses, entertained by the generous hospitality of the last Viscount Scudamore. Here he drew the character of the benevolent John Kyrle, the famous Man of Ross, who with the comparatively small pittance of 500l. a year, diffused comfort and happiness through a large district of country; and effected works of public convenience that would have done honour to a prince:

> Who hung with woods yon mountain's sultry brow?
> From the dry rock who bade the waters flow?
> Whose causeway parts the vale with shady rows?
> Whose seats the weary traveller repose?
> Who taught that heaven-directed spire to rise?
> *The Man of Ross*, each lisping babe replies.

Hom-Lacy is indeed a situation calculated for the poet; inspiration seems to breathe around: in Pope's own language,

> Here waving groves a chequer'd scene display,
> And part admit, and part exclude the day.

Whilst the crystalline Wye, that flows beneath the mansion, forms an enlivening contrast to the solemn shade of these academic bowers.

The house is furnished in an appropriate style of heavy magnificence, and the wainscoating and floors, which are formed of dark wood, assimilate well with every other circumstance in and about it. Several good family portraits of the Scudamores by old masters are displayed in the grand saloon; and a noble picture painted by Hamilton, 16 feet in height, hangs over the chimney-piece. The subject is a very happy one for the banquetting-room in which it is placed: Solomon entertaining the Queen of Sheba. The likenesses of his

Grace in the character of the King of Israel, his Duchess in that of the Queen, and the Honourable Mr. Howard, and Lady E. Bingham, as guests at the table, are well preserved. The exquisite carved work of Gibbons, also, which ornaments the chimney-pieces, and imitates in wood the nice *minutiæ* of nature in the formation of her fruit, plants, and birds, is an object of great curiosity.

We were induced to stroll to the parsonage house of Hom-Lacy in order to survey a pear-tree growing near it, which affords an example of extraordinary fruitfulness. Incredible as the account may appear to be, it is still a serious fact, that this tree has produced for many years the quantity of 14, 15, and 16 hogsheads of perry every season. The respectable incumbent, Mr. Bagnell, (a canon residentiary of Hereford) who has held the living of Hom-Lacy upwards of half a century, attests the fact, and explains it in the following manner: Some years since a large branch being broken down by the wind, its head fell to the ground, the but of it still adhering to the trunk. It was unnoticed for a considerable time; at length, on examination, it appeared to have struck into the ground, taken root, and formed a scion. Willing to humour this *lusus naturæ*, the incumbent gave directions for other layers to be made from the tree in a similar manner; they all took and bore fruit, the parent tree and its offspring now cover a quarter of an acre, and repay the experiment with the enormous product before mentioned. From the church we descended to the ferry over the Wye, opposite to the Duke's house, at the bottom of an extensive meadow. It was not without some alarm that we performed this short voyage, the boats used for the purpose being extremely unsafe. They are long, narrow, flat-bottomed, and worked by a lad, who sits at the stern, and directs it with a paddle. In this little vehicle the passenger is conveyed over a stream always rapid, and frequently, when swollen with rain, extremely agitated and turbulent; thus situated it is absolutely necessary for him to be perfectly motionless, for should he change his position, the cockling boat would inevitably overset, and whelm him in the river, which is here very deep.

Passing the village of Fownhope, we climbed the woody banks of Caplar hill, whose summit exhibits a specimen of Roman castrametation, and commands a pleasing view of the vagarious river winding at its foot. Here it makes a capricious turn to the south, and leads the pedestrian, who follows its banks, a circuitous walk of six miles, to a village called How-Caple, to which a direct path, of only two miles, would carry him, if he choose to leave the course of the Wye. We were, however, much gratified by including this sweep of the river in our walk, as several beautiful points of view, formed by the varied features of its banks, opened to us in our progress through it.

Armstone, the pleasing residence of Mr. Woodhouse; Fawley-Court, (another specimen of the architecture of Queen Elizabeth's time) the family-seat of Mr. Money; the picturesque village of How-Caple, famed for its excellent cider; and Carthage, the house of Mr. Lloyd; successively present themselves as varieties in this agreeable deviation from the usual path. We passed through Ross, which offers nothing of consequence to the observation of the traveller, and proceeded to Wilton, our present quarters. It was formerly a barony, from which the Greys de Wilton took their title. The ancient castle, built in the reign of Henry I. is still existing, and lends its ruins to add to the variety, and heighten the beauty of the magic scenery of this place.

Your's, &c.

R. W.

Letter XVII

TO THE SAME

DEAR SIR,   *Tintern, Aug. 30th.*

ur expedition hastens to a termination, but accident has fortunately led us to finish it with a very agreeable climax. Nothing, indeed, can exceed the beauty of the banks of this romantic river. The scenery, though not stupendous is often grand, sometimes sublime, and never uninteresting. Repeated descriptions of it have been given to the world; but the elegant pen of Mr. Gilpin, directed by taste, and enlivened by fancy, seems alone to have done justice to its inexhaustible and beautiful varieties. Our friend and conductor, Mr. Wathen, met us according to promise this morning at eight o'clock, and shortly after his arrival we began our walk. It was rendered particularly agreeableby a perpetual interchange of cloud and sunshine through the whole day, which gave great effect to the features of the country, by throwing them into transient gloom, and lighting them up with occasional gleams. The first object that engaged our attention was Goodrich Castle, the ancient family-seat of the Talbots, which rises on the opposite bank of the river, at the distance of four miles from Wilton. Crossing the ferry, we ascended to its magnificent remains. They are highly picturesque, and particularly striking, richly decorated with ivy, and "bosomed high in tufted trees;" the crumbling turrets of the massive walls, and the waving heads of the surrounding wood, reflecting a reciprocal charm on each other, form a combination extremely agreeable to the imagination, and impressive to the mind. The architecture is evidently of different ages; specimens of the Anglo-Norman style occur in the windows of the keep, and examples of the pure Gothic (which was a century later) in other parts of the ruins, Quitting the lofty situation of Goodrich Castle, which commands an extensive prospect, we proceeded to Hensham ferry, leaving to the left a considerable sweep of the river, as it contains no features particularly interesting. Having again crossed the Wye, we turned immediately into a path, thro' the meadows on its banks. Here the scene becomes truly majestic. The Coldwell rocks rising to a towering height on the right hand, alternately start through the thick woods which mantle their sides, in lofty, pointed crags; and display broad masses of their surface, relieved by creeping lichens, and diversified with mineral tinges. The little cottages scattered at their feet, the neat residences of industrious labour, form a pleasing accompaniment; exhibiting simplicity contrasted with majesty. Our course led us up a steep and winding ascent (during which we caught occasional views of great beauty) to the summit of Simond's rock, a stupendous precipice, said to be 900 feet above the bed of the river. From hence the river which we have just crossed, with all its contiguous scenery, appears spread beneath us to the north. In an opposite direction are seen the New Weir, the iron-works upon it, a sharp and capricious turn of the river, the Doward rocks, and an huge isolated crag, lifting its detached, precipitous form, crowned with moss, and sprinkled with ivy, to a height little inferior to the cliff from whence it is seen. At the New Weir it was again necessary for us to cross this winding stream, and we continued to follow its meanders, having on our right hand, for better than half a mile, a bold steep bank, covered with noble beech trees, whose deep shade is occasionally relieved by the white face of the rock discov-

ered through it. The Doward rocks, which constitute a very grand feature of the Wye, now began
to open upon us, and the effect produced upon
the imagination by their towering stratified appearance, is much enlivened by the circumstance
of a fine echo, the *centrum phonicum* of which
appears to be near a spreading beech tree in the
middle of the meadow. Our path quickly led us
to the turnpike road from Ross to Monmouth,
which runs parallel with the river for some distance, and commands a glorious view of the Wye,
with its rough rocks, and luxuriant woods! We
hastened through the neat town of Monmouth,
built on the confluence of the rivers Wye and
Monnow, and passing the bridge thrown over
the latter, turned again into the meadows near its
margin. At the distance of little better than half
a mile from Monmouth, the river makes another grand sweep to the right, and assumes a different character from that which it has hitherto
observed. Dismissing its rocks and precipices, it
rolls through lofty sloping hills, thickly covered
with waving woods from their roots to their tops.
All here is solemn, still, and soothing; a deep
repose reigns around, and attunes the mind to
meditation. An agreeable variety, however; soon
occurs, the little picturesque village of Redbrook,
a bustling, busy scene, enlivened by active industry in various forms. White-Brook, another
hamlet, ornamented with the house of General
Rooke, presently succeeds; to the left of which,

on a commanding elevation, is seen the village of St. Brieval's with its church and castle, the latter serving as a prison for those convicted of trespasses in the neighbouring forest of Dean. It is difficult to give a just idea of the singular village of Llandogo, that now opens upon us. You must imagine, my dear sir, a lofty hill, whose indented side is mantled with deep woods, through which a multitude of small cottages, sprinkled over the declivity in an artless, whimsical, and picturesque manner, shew their little whitened fronts, and strongly impress the imagination with the idea of its being fairy land, the romantic residence of Oberon, Mab, and their fantastic train. This spot is generally esteemed, and with great justice, a beautiful feature of the Wye. The river now takes a sharp turn to the left, and hurrying on half a mile further to Cardithel, experiences a considerable and singular depression of its level, sinking, gradually, several feet. Passing thro' the populous village of Brookweir, to which the Severn hoys ascend in order to receive the lading of the Wye barges, we left for a short time the banks of the river, and wound up a narrow lane for another mile. We then attained the summit of a hill, and a prospect immediately burst upon us, scarcely to be equalled for richness and variety. Behind us lay the fairy region of Llandogo, the busy village of Brookweir deeply embosomed in wood, and the crystalline river, studded with vessels of different descriptions. Before us were spread the village of Tintern, with the diversified scenery of the dale in which it stands, its glittering stream and dark woods, and the lofty ruins of its abbey, a beautiful Gothic pile rising in solemn majesty, spotted with mosses, and crowned with ivy. The whole scene was gloriously tinted by the rich illumination of a setting sun.

We slowly descended the hill, indulging the reflections which the view had inspired, and crossing the Wye for the last time, proceeded to the Beaufort Arms, a very comfortable inn, kept by Mr. Gething, the antiquary and historian of the village.

Your's, &c.

R. W.

Letter XVIII

TO THE SAME

DEAR SIR, *Chepstow, Aug. 31st.*

hilst we are waiting for the flood tide in order to cross the Severn, on our return to Bath, I indulge myself in troubling you with a few additional lines, as a finish to the slight account of our expedition, which, in compliance with your request, I have attempted to give you. The brevity I must necessarily observe in my concluding letter, will, I apprehend, need the less apology, as the scenery of this place and its neighbourhood has already been described by Tourists out of number, who have been so particular in their details, as to leave nothing to be gleaned by such birds of passage as C—— and myself.

The extreme heat of the last night effectually prevented us from sleeping, and we passed the greater part of it at our window. This we were induced to do both for the sake of a balmy and refreshing breeze that gently whispered without, and in order to enjoy a scene perfectly new tous, highly gratifying to a warm imagination. Immediately opposite to the room in which we were lodged stands a large iron forge, one amongst the many that are constantly worked night and day, in the valley of Tintern. The wide folding-doors were thrown open, and as they faced our window, the interior part of the edifice, with its huge apparatus, and the operations carried on by it, were displayed to our view. Here the dingy beings who melt the ore, and prepare it for the bar hammer, were seen busied in their horrible employment, all the detail of which we clearly discovered by the assistance of the strong illumination cast on them from the flaming furnaces. This scene of bustle amidst smoke and fire, during the darkness and silence of midnight, which was only interrupted by the intonations of the bar-hammer, produced a most impressive effect on the mind. We saw Virgil's description realized, and the interior of Etna, the forges of the Cyclops, and their fearful employment, immediately occurred to us.

Fulgores nunc terrificos, sonitumque, metumque
Miscebant operi, flammisque sequacibus iras.
——Gemit impositis, incudibus antrum.
Illi inter sese multâ vi brachia tollunt
In numerum, versantque tenaci forcipe massam.

EN, viii. 431.

Our impatience to survey the ruins of Tintern abbey induced us to rise with the sun. It was some time, however, before we were gratified, for the key of it having been very injudiciously taken from Mr. Gething, and placed in the hands of a man on the other side of the river, considerable delay and trouble arise in procuring it; an inconvenience which is not recompensed by the civility of the ciceroni, who has none of the obliging attention of our host at the Beaufort Arms. After much vociferation, we at length gained the key, and were admitted into the abbey. The *coup d'oeil*, on opening the western entrance, is, unquestionably, very fine. The peculiar elegance and lightness of all its members immediately strike the eye. Nothing, indeed, can be more perfect than the architecture of its various parts; its moulded arches, clustering pillars, and figured windows. Nature, also, as if to render the ruin compleat, has taken abundant pains in decorating its columns and walls with a profuse coating of ivy, which is very happily contrasted to the light hue of the stone used in the building, that even now preserves much of its original whiteness. This beautiful ruin is cruciform, two hundred and thirty feet in length, and thirty-three in breadth; the transept stretches north and south one hundred and sixty feet. It was originally the great church belonging to the Cistertian Abbey of Tintern, founded by Walter de Clare in 1131, and dedicated to St. Mary, as all monasteries of that order were. Falling a prey to the rapacity of Henry VIII. at the dissolution, (when its estates amounted to 1921. *per annum*) it was granted by him in 1537 to the Earl of Worcester. Many vestiges of other buildings belonging to the abbey may be traced, such as door-ways, shafts of pillars, &c. and they all prove that the purest stile of Gothic architecture was observed in the structure of the great church and the contiguous edifices. Having gratified ourselves with a minute observation of every part of this ruin, and visited the iron-works, where the crude ore is melted, and formed into rough pigs, preparatory to its being manufactured, we bade farewell to our kind friend Wathen, (who returned to Hereford) and took the road towards Chepstow. One other grand view remained to us before we finished our expedition; I mean that which is seen from a stupendous elevation called the Wine-cliff, (a corruption, probably, of Wye-cliff) rising a little to the north-east of Piercefield, and overlooking the surrounding country. Quitting the road, and taking a path through the meadows to the left hand, we reached this eminence by a gradual ascent, and were suddenly astonished with a scene grand and unbounded. Immediately under the cliff is seen the Wye, following a course the most whimsical and sinuous that can be conceived, and discharging its waters into the Severn at Chepstow. The vast mural, lime-stone precipices, that rise abruptly from its banks, finely diversified by a regular alternation of rock and wood, appear in front and to the left. Piercefield, with all its magic scenery, lies under to the eye, to the right. Beyond it the ruined castle of Chepstow, and its busy town, are caught. And in the distance, the straining vision roves over Glocestershire, Somersetshire, and Monmouthshire, and following the course of the magnificent Severn, is at length lost in the Bristol Channel.

Not being fortunate enough to gain admission into the grounds of Piercefield, for this is not a day of their public exhibition, we walked on towards Chepstow, through a country extremely pleasing. The name of this town, according to Camden, signifies a "place of trading," and it still retains some appearance of its ancient celebrity in that respect. It is built on the Wye, about two miles from the point where it discharges itself into the Severn, and is provided with proper quays for the convenience of the numerous vessels which frequent the place. A wooden bridge of prodigious height, erected on piles, crosses the river to the south of the town. The boards which form the flooring of this are not fastened, but so disposed as to rise and fall with the tide, which is known sometimes to exceed seventy feet in height. The church is a curious edifice. It formerly belonged to the alien Benedictine priory of Strigule, but was converted at the Reformation into the parish church of Chepstow. The æra of its erection may be pretty well ascertained by the circular arches and massive Anglo-Norman pillars of the great aisle, together with the western door, which exhibits a beautiful and perfect specimen of the architecture of the eleventh century. But the glory of Chepstow is its ruined castle, "mighty in decay," and occupying a great extent of ground. This also dates its origin from the early Norman times, and was probably erected immediately subsequent to the Conquest. We entered it by a lofty gateway of noble appearance, and surveyed with wonder its extensive remains, and substantial walls. Founded on a bold, perpendicular rock, and constructed with all the strength which art could bestow upon it, Chepstow Castle bade fair to boast an endurance equal to the firm basis on which it is built. The fallen turrets, however, and dilapidated walls, crumbling gradually into annihilation, evince the impossibility of resisting the silent, but uninterrupted attacks of Time, who sooner or later levels with the dust all the monuments of human vanity, and all the efforts of human labour.

> And e'en so fares it with the things of earth
> Which seem most constant: there will come the cloud

That shall enfold them up, and leave their place
A seat for emptiness. Our narrow ken
Reaches too far, when all that we behold
Is but the havock of wide-wasting Time,
Or what he soon shall spoil. His outspread wings
(Which bear him like an eagle o'er the earth)
Are plum'd in front so downy soft, they seem
To foster what they touch, and mortal fools
Rejoice beneath their hovering: woe the while!
For in that indefatigable flight
The multitudinous strokes incessantly
Bruise all beneath their cope, and mark on all
His secret injury; on the front of man
Greyhairs and wrinkles; still as Time speeds on,
Hard and more hard his iron pennons beat
With ceaseless violence; nor overpass,
Till all the creatures of this nether world
Are one wide quarry: following dark behind,
The cormorant Oblivion swallows up
The carcasses that Time has made his prey.

Your's, &c.

R. W.

Index

Æ

Æneid (Virgil) 35
Æthelfrith 122

A

Abergavenny xiii, 21, 22, 24,
    25, 26
Aberglaslyn 102
Abergwilly, College of 32
Aberystwyth 54, 132
Adriatic Sea 58
*A Gentleman's Tour Through
    Monmouthshire and
    Wales* (Wyndham) 101
Agricola, Gnaeus Julius 12
Alps 58

Anacreon 157
Angel Inn, Abergavenny 23
Angel Inn, Rhaeadr Gwy 48
Anglesey 119
Anglo Norman princes 11
Anne, Queen of Great Britain
    184
Ansbach, Alexander, Margrave
    of Brandenburg- 145
Antoninus Pius, Titus Aelius
    Hadrianus 19, 25
Apennines 58
Armstone 195
Arundel family 176
Ashmole, Elias 38
Augustine of Canterbury 122

B

Bagnell, Mr (canon residentiary of Hereford) 193
Baldwin of Flanders 172
Baldwin, Thomas 53
Bangor xiv, 119, 120, 121, 122, 123, 124
Bangor Bridge 123
Bard, The (Gray) 129
Barmouth 101
Baron Hill, Anglesea 120
Bath xii, xiii, xv, 4, 5, 13, 51, 53, 203
Beaufort Arms, Crickhowell 28
Beaufort Arms, Tintern 202, 205
Beddgelert 87, 103
Benedictine Nuns 19
Bernard de Neufmarché 32
Berwyn Range 143, 144, 168
Bingham, E. 193
Bishop's Castle 176
Bodenham, Charles 190
Bohun, House of 32
Bovium 122
Bradford, Henry Bridgeman, 1st Baron 168
Brampton Brian xiv, 178, 179
Brampton, Brian 178
Brampton, Bryan de 178
Brampton, Margaret de 178
Braose, House of 32
Brecknock Castle 32
Brecknock, Lord of 32
Brecknockshire 36, 46
Brecon xiii, 21, 27, 29, 31, 38
Breidden Hill 168
Bristol 5, 26, 207

Bristol Channel 207
Britons 2, 24, 27, 30, 78, 118, 122, 139, 154
Brochwel Ysgithrog 122
Brookweir 201
Buckingham, Duke of, Humphrey Stafford. *See* Stafford, Henry, 2nd Duke of Buckingham
Bulkeley, Thomas James
Bulkeley, 7th Viscount 120
Burrell, 1st Baron Gwydyr, Peter 136
Burrium 19
Butler, 5th Earl of Ormond, James 186
Butler, Eleanor 151

C

Cader Idris xiv, 2, 71, 79, 80, 81, 83, 84, 85, 90, 110
Cadwgan ap Bleddyn ap Cynfyn 171
Caernarfon xiv, 101, 105, 108, 109, 114, 115, 116, 118, 119, 134
Caernarfon Castle 115
Caernarfonshire 4, 84, 137, 164
Caerwent xiii, 10, 12, 15
Cæsar, Julius 154
Caldicot Castle 10, 11, 12
Cambrians 28, 133
Camden, William 29, 140, 207
Canterbury 33
Capel Voelas xiv, 137
Caplar Hill 194
Cardigan Bay 101

Cardiganshire 3, 57, 60
Cardithel 201
Carmarthenshire 26
Carreg-y-Gwalch 136
Carthage 195
Cassiterides 78
Castle Green 190
Castle Inn, Wigmore 180
Castle Rising 176
Cayne, River xiv, 93, 95
Ceiriog, River 162
Celts 28, 154
Cernioge xiv, 139, 142
Cerrigydrudion 139, 141
Charles VI of France 88
Charlton family, Shropshire
    172
Cheapside 46
Chepstow xv, 15, 16, 175, 190,
    203, 206, 207, 208
Chepstow Castle 208
Cheshire 161
Chester 84, 123, 132, 160
Chirk Castle 150, 161, 162
Cicero 2
Cistertians 89, 148, 206
Clare, Walter de 206
Clee Hills 84
Clifton 84
Clive, 1st Earl of Powis, Ed-
    ward 176
Clun xiv, 175, 176, 177
Clun Castle 176
Clwyd 2
Clytha Castle 22
Coldwell Rocks 199
Colwyn, River 103
Comus (Milton) 9
Conwy xiv, 45, 77, 117, 124,

126, 128, 129, 132, 134,
    135, 136, 137
Conwy Castle 127, 132, 133,
    134
Conwy, River 135
Corwen xiv, 143
Craig-Cae 82
Creyddyn 126
Crickhowell xiii, 26, 27
Crickhowell Castle 27
Crispinus 38
Cumberland, Richard 58
Cwm-Llan 107
Cwm-y-Cae 81
Cwm-Ysom 93
Cwmystwyth 54
Cymer (Kemmer) Abbey 89
Cynric Rwth 140

D

Dean Forest 201
Dee, River 123
Denbighshire 137
Devil's Bridge 57, 59, 61, 66,
    69, 71, 103
Dinas-Bran xiv, 144, 145, 148,
    149, 150, 162
Dinas-Bran Castle 145, 150
Dinâs-Emrys 106
Diodorus 154, 157
dissolution of the monasteries
    25, 89, 185
Dolbadern Castle xiv, 112, 113
Dolgellau xiv, 75, 85, 88, 91,
    92
Dolydd-Cae 80
Dôl-y-Myllyn xiv, 2, 91
Dovey (Dyfi), River 2, 72, 77
Doward rocks 199, 200

Drayton, Michael 123
Druids 27, 119, 140
Dwy'ryd, River 101
Dyflàs, River 78
Dyndor Hill 190

E

Edward III of England 124
Edward I of England 45, 118, 132, 133
Eleanor of Castile 118
Elizabeth I of England and Ireland 172, 190, 195
Ellesmere Canal 169
Ely 32, 33
Ely tower 33
Etna, Mount 204
Evans, Mrs (hostess at the Angel Inn, Rhaeadr Gwy) 48

F

Faërie Queene (Spenser) 124
Festiniogg 2
Ffestiniog 101
Ffestiniog Valley 99, 100
Fillan 156
Fitzalan Earls of Arundel 150
FitzOsbern, 1st Earl of Hereford, William 184
Fitzroy, Charles 191
FitzWalter, Miles, 1st Earl of Hereford 25
Fownhope 194
Francton, Adam de 45

G

Gam, Sir David 72
Gething, Mr (innkeeper of the

Beaufort Arms, Tintern) 202, 205
Gibbons, Grinling 193
Giffard, John 45
Gilpin, William 197
Giraldus Cambrensis 25
Glisseg rocks 144, 149
Glocestershire 26, 27, 207
Glynn, River 142
Golden Lion, Dolgellau 85
Goodrich Castle xv, 198
Gray, Thomas 129
Great Orme 120
Greeks 35
Grey de Wilton family 195
Grey, Thomas 135
Griffiths, William (former tenant at Llan Farm nr Caernarfon) 108
Gruffydd II ap Madog, Lord of Dinas Bran 150
Gruffydd II ap Madog, Lord of Dinas Bran 162
Guatirs 142
Guendolen 9
Gwenwynwyn ab Owain Cyfeiliog 171
Gwydir Castle 136
Gwydyr, Peter Burrell, 1st Baron 136

H

Hafôd 53, 57, 59, 63, 70
Hafod Arms, Devil's Bridge, Ceredigion 60, 63, 70
Hall, Harry 179
Hamelin de Ballon 25
Hamilton, William 192

Hand Inn, Llangollen 145, 150
Hanmer, John 88
Harlech Castle 101
Harley, 5th Earl of Oxford and Earl Mortimer, Edward 178, 184
Harley family 178
Harley, Thomas 184
Henry III of England 89
Henry II of England 143
Henry I of England 32, 195
Henry IV 33, 73, 102, 113
Henry VII 11
Henry VIII 32, 148, 149, 206
Herbert, George Edward Henry Arthur, 2nd Earl of Powys 172
Hereford xv, 25, 175, 179, 183, 184, 186, 189, 190, 193, 206
Hereford, 1st Earl of, Miles FitzWalter of Gloucester. *See* FitzWalter, Miles, 1st Earl of Hereford
Herefordshire 27, 176
Hereford, William FitzOsbern, 1st Earl of 184
Herle, Robert de 178
Hogarth, William 48
Hom Lacy 190, 191, 192, 193
Honddu, River 33
Houris 128
How Caple 194, 195
Humphries, Siôn 126
Hutchings, Mr (inkeeper at Three Eagles, Bangor) 120

I

Ireland 83, 110
Isle of Man 84

Isle of Wight 78
Israel 193
Itinerarium Antonini Augusti (Antoninus) 19
Itinerary (Leland) 11

J

Joel (prophet) 111
Johnes, Thomas 53, 57, 59, 60
Jones, Edward 80
Jones, Inigo 114, 136
Jones, Mr (harp player at the Bull Inn, Conway) 129, 132
Jones, William (Presbyterian cleric) 98

K

Kemmer (Cymer) Abbey 89
King's Head Inn, Caernarfon 116
Kistvaen 140
Knox, John 179
Kyrle, John 191

L

Lake of Three Grains 85
Lambert, John 162
Lancastrians 186
Lancester, House of 186
Langollen 2
Leland, John 11, 15, 149, 176
Letty (wife of Robert Lewis, haymaker) 41
Lewis, Robert (haymaker nr Raeadr Gwy) 40, 41
Lion, The, Brecon 36, 49
Little Orme 120

Liverpool 132
Livy 154
Llanberis 112, 113, 114, 157
Llandogo xv, 201
Llandygai 124
Llan Egwest 144
Llaneltyd 89, 91, 96
Llanfair 17, 18, 126
Llan Farm 108
Llangollen xiv, 139, 143, 144,
    145, 149, 151, 159, 160, 161
Llangollen Vale 151
Llanidlos 70
Llanrwst 136, 137
Llanymynach xiv, 164, 167,
    168, 169, 170
Lloyd, Mr 195
Lloyd, William (guide) 106
Llyn Cae 82
Llyn Cau 84
Llyn Dinas 106
Llyn-Gafr 85
Llyn-Mullyn 85
Llyn Padarn 114
Llywelyn ab Iorwerth 73, 113
Llywelyn ap Gruffudd 45, 89
Locrine 9
London 38, 46, 75, 109
Lords Marchers 176

M

Mab 201
Machynlleth 70, 72, 77, 79
Madox, William 91
Maentwrog 88, 99
Man of Ross 191, 192
March, Edmund Mortimer,
    2nd Baron Mortimer of
    Wigmore 173

Margaret of Anjou 186
Mawddach, River xiv, 2, 89,
    90, 93, 94, 95
Mawddach Valley 93
Menai Strait 119, 120
Mercia 163
Merddin Emrys 106
Merioneth 4, 60, 101, 137,
    154, 164
Merionethshire 77, 79, 123
Merionethshire mountains 79
Merlin 106, 124
Mictis 78
Minffordd, Tallyllyn 79
Moina 24
Mona 134
Money, Mr 195
Monmouth xv, 200
Monnow, River 200
Montgomery 172, 175
Montgomeryshire 47, 60
Moreton, John (Bishop of Ely)
    32, 33
Mortimer, Edmund 45
Mortimer, Edmund, 2nd Bar-
    on Mortimer of Wigmore
    173
Mortimer family 173, 184
Mortimer, Roger 162
Mortimer's Cross, Battle of 186
Mortimer's Cross, nr Wigmore
    186
Mortimer, Sir Hugh de 185
Myddelton, Charlotte 150, 162
Myddelton family 162
Myddelton, Richard 162
Myddelton, Sir Thomas 172,
    173
Mynach, River 60, 61, 62

N

Nereus 10
New Forest 1
New Passage xv, 6, 7, 8, 175
New Weir xv, 199
Norfolk, Charles Howard, 11th
    Duke of 190, 191, 194
Normans 11, 25, 32, 172, 176,
    178, 198, 208
Northumbrians 163
Notitia Monastica (Tanner)
    25

O

Oakley, William 99
Oberon 201
Ogwen, River 124
Ordovices 2
Ormond, Earl of Wiltshire,
    James Butler, 5th Earl of
    186
Ossian 47, 120, 131, 156
Ostorius Scapula, Publius 9
Oswald of Northumbria 163
Oswestry xiv, 161, 163
Owain Glyndwr 72, 73, 88,
    113
Owain Goch ap Gruffydd 113
Oxford and Earl Mortimer,
    Edward Harley, 5th Earl of
    178, 179, 184

P

Paget, 2nd Earl of Uxbridge,
    Henry 120
Paris 103
Parlamentarians 173
Parliament, House of 125
Parry, Harry 114
Pembrokeshire 26, 84
Penda of Mercia 163
Penmaenmaur 67, 120, 125
Penmorfa 101
Pennant, 1st Baron Penrhyn,
    Richard 114
Pennant, Thomas 134
Pennervaen 38
Penrhyn Castle 124
Penrhyn, Richard Pennant, 1st
    Baron 114
Pentre 57
Pen-yr-Cader 84
Percy, Thomas 42
Piercefield 206, 207
Pistil-y-Cayne 93
Pistily-Mawddach 94
Plâs Newydd, Anglesey 119
Plas Newydd, Llangollen 151
Plimhimmon 60, 71
Ponsonby, Sarah 151
Pont-aber-glas-Lyn 101
Pont-ar-Diawl 61
Pont-ar-Garfa 92
Pont-ar-Mynach 61
Pont-ar-wyd 71
Pont Fawr, Llanrwst 136
Pont-y-Swlty 160
Pope, Alexander 191
Porthleyd 135
Powis Castle xiv, 170
Powys, Kingdom of 122
Presteign 177
Priestholme Island 120
Prince of Wales's mountain
    92
Puffin's Island 120

Pughe, David 80, 81

R

Radnorshire 45, 46
Reliques of Ancient English Poetry (Percy) 42
Rhaeadr Gwy xiii, 37, 38, 39, 46, 51, 52, 53, 56
Rheidol, River 63, 71
Rhine 58
Rhythallt, River 114
Richard III 32
Richard II of England 73
Roberts, Henry 90
Romans 2, 12, 15, 16, 17, 19, 29, 118, 122, 135, 146, 168, 190, 194
Rooke, James 200
Rosa, Salvator 102
Ross-on-Wye 186, 190, 195, 200
Rotherwas 190
Runic circles 16
Ruthin 145

S

Sabine Hills 58
Salmon Leap 102
Salop 84, 176
Saxon architecture 16
Scethrog 31
Scottish Highlands 156
Scudamore family 191, 192
Scudamore, Frances 193
Scudamore, James Scudamore, 3rd Viscount 191
Scudamore, Philip de 191
Segontium 118

Severn, River xiii, xv, 1, 8, 9, 10, 11, 26, 71, 172, 201, 203, 207
Shakespeare, William 73
Sheba, Queen of 192
Shrewsbury 160
Shropshire 161, 169, 172, 177
Silures 2
Simond's rock 199
Skeffington, Thomas (Bishop of Bangor) 120
Skirrid Fawr (Welsh: Ysgyryd Fawr) 26
Snowdon xiv, 2, 67, 71, 83, 103, 105, 106, 108, 109, 113, 136
Solomon 192
Somerset 26
Somerset, 2nd Earl of Worcester, Henry 206
Spenser, Edmund 124
Spring: A Poem (Thomson) 11
Stafford, Henry, 2nd Duke of Buckingham 32, 33
St Austin, Order of 185
St Brieval's 201
St Clare family 19
St David's 84
St David's, Bishop of. *See* Stuart, William (Bishop of St David's)
St Mary 206
Strabo 29, 154
Strata Florida Abbey 61
St Scudamore 191
Stuart, William (Bishop of St David's) 32
St Vincent at Mans 25
Swansea 84

Switzerland 58
Sydney Gardens 6
Sylvester, Charles 125

T

Tacitus 9
Talbot family 198
Tall-y-llyn 79
Tanner, Thomas 25
Tan-y-Bwlch xiv, 99, 100
Tan-y Bwlch Hall 99
Tan-y-Bwlch Inn 100
Thomas, Ann 126
Thomson, James 11, 63
Three Eagles Inn, Bangor 120
Three-Salmons Inn, Usk 19
Timon's Villa (Pope) 171
Tintern xv, 187, 197, 202,
    204, 205, 206
Tintern Abbey 187, 201, 206
Traeth Bach, 101
Tudor, Jasper, 7th Earl of
    Pembroke 186
Turkey 16
Tylyn Gwladys 93
Tyrol 58

U

Usk xiii, 1, 17, 19, 22, 36, 77
Usk Castle 19
Usk, River 19
Uxbridge, Henry Paget, 2nd
    Earl of 120

V

Valle Crucis Abbey 144, 145,
    146
Virgil 9, 35, 204

Vortigern 106
Vrond Farm, Llangollen 161
Vyrnwy, River 170

W

Walter, Hubert (Archbishop of
    Canterbury) 171
Warenne, John de, 6th Earl of
    Surrey 150, 162
Warren, John (Bishop of Ban-
    gor) 121
Wathen, Mr 190
Welshpool 169, 170
Westbury 5
White Brook 200
Wicklow Mountains 110
Wigmore xv, 175, 177, 178,
    180, 183, 184, 185, 186
Wigmore Abbey 185
Wigmore Castle 183, 184
William de Braose 25
William of Hereford 25
William the Conqueror 25,
    119, 172
Wilton xv, 186, 189, 195, 198
Wilton Bridge, Ross-on-Wye
    186
Wiltshire 26
Wnion, River 88
Woodhouse, Mr 195
Worcester, Henry Somerset,
    2nd Earl of 206
Wrekin, The 84
Wrexham 84
Wu, River 106
Wyatt, Samuel 124
Wye, River xv, 46, 52, 71, 175,
    186, 190, 192, 194, 199,
    200, 201, 202, 206, 207

Wyndham, Henry Penrud-
    docke 101
Wynne Arms, Machynlleth 72
Wynne family 137
Wynne, Sir W. W. 103
Wynnestay 161

Y

Yale 150, 162
Y Aran 106, 107
Y Lliwedd 106
Yonge, Griffith 88
York, House of 186
Yrth St. Collen ap Gwynnawg
    ap Clydawg ap Cowrda
    ap Caradog Freichfras ap
    Lleyr Merim ap Einion ap
    Cunedda Wledig 160
Ysgyryd Fawr (English: Skirrid
    Fawr) 26
Ystwyth, River 53

Milton Keynes UK
Ingram Content Group UK Ltd.
UKHW040741301124
451843UK00016B/277/J